THE ESSENTIAL

Hoihnu Hauzel is a native of Manipur. She completed her schooling in Shillong and Delhi, and has a master's degree in political science from Delhi University. She has been a journalist for the last fifteen years and has worked with the *Asian Age*, *Indian Express*, *Hindustan Times*, the *Times of India*, and the *Telegraph* in Delhi. She is currently pursuing an independent writing career and continues to promote the North-East through her writings and entrepreneurial ventures like her travel portal, Northeast Odyssey (www.northeastodyssey.com) and a digital North-East lifestyle magazine, *NE Travel and Life* (www.netravelandlife.com).

She has also to her credit a book of poems, *Moments of Time*. Hoihnu is committed to the development of the North-East. This book is, for her, a step towards the promotion of the region. Her coffee-table book on Manipur is set to be released next year.

The ESSENTIAL NORTH-EAST *Cookbook*

HOIHNU HAUZEL

PENGUIN BOOKS
An imprint of Penguin Random House

PENGUIN BOOKS

USA | Canada | UK | Ireland | Australia
New Zealand | India | South Africa | China | Singapore

Penguin Books is part of the Penguin Random House group of companies whose addresses can be found at global.penguinrandomhouse.com

Published by Penguin Random House India Pvt. Ltd
4th Floor, Capital Tower 1, MG Road,
Gurugram 122 002, Haryana, India

Penguin Random House India

First published by Penguin Books India 2003
This revised edition published 2014

Copyright © Hoihnu Hauzel 2003, 2014

All rights reserved

10 9 8 7 6 5 4 3 2

ISBN 9780143423881

Typeset in Myriad Pro by Eleven Arts, Delhi
Printed at Manipal Technologies Limited, India

This book is sold subject to the condition that it shall not, by way of trade or otherwise, be lent, resold, hired out, or otherwise circulated without the publisher's prior consent in any form of binding or cover other than that in which it is published and without a similar condition including this condition being imposed on the subsequent purchaser.

www.penguin.co.in

This is a legitimate digitally printed version of the book and therefore might not have certain extra finishing on the cover.

I dedicate this book to my late paternal grandfather, Taivel Hauzel, who first introduced me to the aroma of roasted meat, and to my late maternal grandfather, T. Twalchin, who will always remind me that 'having a good appetite to enjoy food is a blessing from God'

Contents

Acknowledgements	ix
Introduction	xi
Culture and Food Habits	xi
Speciality Ingredients	xix
Table of Measures	xxii
ARUNACHAL PRADESH	1
Feasts from the Tribal Kitchen	3
ASSAM	23
Meals from the Banks of the Brahmaputra	25
MANIPUR	57
Titbits from Loktak Valley	59
MEGHALAYA	77
Delectable Treats from the Khasi Hills	79
MIZORAM	99
Delicacies from the Mizo Hills	101
NAGALAND	123
Recipes from Jhapfu Mountain	125

TRIPURA	147
Dishes from the Tripuri Kitchen	149
SIKKIM	163
The Secret of the Sikkimese Kitchen	165
Glossary	191
Index	195

Acknowledgements

To write a book on the cuisine, culture and customs of the North-East has not been an easy task, simply because there are no written records on the subject. This book has entailed many years of research during which time I have travelled through the states of the North-East and visited the kitchens of the different tribes, to actually see and document their cooking procedures. This comprehensive research was only possible with the help of the elders of the tribes who shared their knowledge with me and gave me hitherto unwritten and unknown information. I thank them all.

I will always be grateful to the many nameless cooks and housewives of different states for helping me with every detail in the art of cooking perfect North-Eastern meals. I thank my wonderful friends in Delhi and Gurgaon for always accepting my invitations to come home and sample my cooking each time I cook something authentic. They have encouraged me to delve deep into the subject and keep my passion alive.

I owe a great debt to the late Dera Natung, the former Education Minister of Arunachal Pradesh, who supplied me with authentic Arunachali ingredients to familiarize me with their aromas. He was enthusiastic about the book till the end; the chapter on Arunachal Pradesh would not have been possible without him.

My thanks to Mr M.P. Bezbaruah, former secretary, Tourism, Ministry of Tourism, and his wife, Mrs Bezbaruah, who often had to forgo their afternoon siesta to go through my manuscript on Assam.

Sanjoy Hazarika, writer and documentary film-maker, gave me free access to his books on the North-East.

Thinlay Topgay, eminent lawyer from Sikkim, helped me with every detail of Sikkimese cooking and was my guide. Binita Rai from Sikkim Tourism, I thank her for her patience in taking me through Nepali cuisine.

My elder sister, Alice, collected valuable material and shared her recipes with me.

Rajesh Khanna, my friend, confidant, guinea pig and beloved husband, for being my best critic when it comes to my cooking. His constant feedback helps me understand what works for most palettes.

Devyani Onial, my former colleague, spent many afternoons looking through my manuscript and giving valuable advice. Manjula Negi, my former colleague and friend, I thank her for fine-tuning my work.

My special thanks go to my parents for their financial and moral support, which made all those trips to the North-East possible and which helped complete my task.

Finally I thank David Davidar, the first publisher of this book, for having faith in me. I also thank Chiki Sarkar and the team at Penguin Books India for their work on both editions of the book.

Introduction

CULTURE AND FOOD HABITS

'Catch a dog, kill it, roast it and eat it, and what you have is a North-East delicacy,' a North Indian friend once remarked jovially. Of course, food from the North-East is much more than just the imagined dog's meat—it boasts exotic delicacies that are not a part of mainstream Indian fare.

The rest of India knows very little about the people and cuisine of North-East India: Assam, Arunachal Pradesh, Meghalaya, Manipur, Mizoram, Nagaland, Tripura and Sikkim. Just like their topographical beauty, the gastronomic fare of the eight states remains by and large hidden from the rest of the country. This segregation has more to do with a lack of marketing than inadequacies in the cuisine itself, and so these delicacies continue to be prepared and appreciated within the confines of their areas.

A lot has changed since the first edition of this book came out in 2004. There was no way for the rest of India to have a glimpse of what food from *that* mystic part of India was. Momos—the true offshoots of the Tibetan influence in Sikkim—were all that people thought food from the North-East was all about. Interestingly, things have changed in the last few years. The evolution of food in India has also brought many regional cuisines of the country to the fore. More importantly, the growing attempt to create a continuous dialogue and build bridges between the North-East and the rest of India has ensured that the food from this region must now travel naturally and inevitably out of its boundaries. This enabled many enterprising food entrepreneurs from the region to gather the courage to open restaurants serving North-Eastern food. Most of them began with the predictable and palatable dishes and slowly graduated to more authentic North-Eastern fare. These offerings are not lapped up only by homesick North-Easterners. Rather, a growing tribe of converts who are willing to experiment with different flavours have kept businesses thriving till date. So, it is no longer just the food pavilions at New Delhi's Dilli Haat that serve food from the North-East.

There is something about the flavour from this region that is slowly gaining ground and acceptance from people outside the region. It's not quite Thai, but close enough to be compared because of the many shared and common ingredients like khang khu—which the Paite tribes in Manipur love and the Thais call cha-om—a leafy green of a tree with a strong peculiar aroma. The flavour of North-Eastern food is somewhat reminiscent of Vietnamese food because it is bland. It can also be compared to Malaysian food because of some of the common ingredients. But the main difference is that Malays use coconut, which people in the North-East have traditionally not had access to, except in Assam where coconut is found in abundance. Considered exotic anyway by gourmet gurus, this simple and healthy but flavourful food that uses natural spices and little oil is finding takers slowly but surely. Food connoisseurs are waking up to the new flavours from the North-East. In their quest for exotic food from different corners of India, many enterprising chefs are more open and willing to experiment with food from this part of the country. We may still conclude that while food from the corner of India has huge potential, what it needs is to be served in the right place with the right selection of dishes.

Food from the North-East is garnering attention which is international as well. Gordon Ramsay came to India to film an episode of *Gordon's Great Escape* and, in a book by the same name, featured two recipes, fish tenga, an Assamese sour fish curry, and Majuli fishcakes with tomato, another local dish of the island, both of which made it to his 100 favourite recipes from India. The celebrated chef, who boasts twelve Michelin stars, headed all the way from London to Nagaland and Assam to find out why Nagas use bamboo shoots in every form: fresh, smoked and dried. He also noticed that people from that region use more natural and fresh spices like chillies, ginger and garlic—not dry spices like the rest of India. And when Italian slow food icon Carlos Petrini came to India, it was in Meghalaya that he bonded with the locals over sumptuous pork curry and the many interesting herbs and spices that he was surprised to see. 'I have never had such delicious food. It is interesting,' Petrini had told the author of this book.

So what is food from North-East all about? The dishes of the North-East are not laced with oil and spices, yet they are delicious, and the locally grown aromatic herbs make them exotic. They are light, healthy and easy to prepare. Simplicity, in fact, is the hallmark of North-Eastern cuisine. The basic components of a meal are steamed or boiled rice, accompanied by a gravy-based meat or fish dish, and a chutney, washed down with a soup of boiled vegetables. The best way to relish a North-Eastern meal is to eat it with your hands. The younger generation may now use spoons and forks, but they return to their roots when they really want to enjoy their meals.

Unlike the oily, rich food prepared in some other parts of India, which is heavy and cannot be eaten all the time, you keep coming back to the bland and barely spiced fare of the North-East. However, it is still an acquired taste, partly because of the lack of spices but also because of the overpowering flavours of some of the ingredients, like the fermented bamboo shoots.

There are differences in the items consumed and the preparation of food among the people of the North-East, based on religion and culture. The tribes not influenced by Hinduism relish meat, while Hindu communities like the Asomiyas of Assam eat fish and mutton, and the Meiteis of Manipur eat fish at the very most. The people of the predominantly Christian states of Nagaland, Mizoram, Meghalaya, and about 40 per cent of the Manipuris, do not have any religious restrictions in their diet. Tribes like the Bodos of Assam consider a meal incomplete without pork, and the tribes of Tripura must have fermented fish to complete their meal.

What further differentiates the people of the North-East from one another is their style of cooking. The food varies from region to region and tribe to tribe. Each of the sixteen Naga tribes, for instance, boasts a distinct delicacy, which is different in flavour and style from that of the other tribes. The Angamis cook a chunky meat dish with raja chillies (jungle chillies) and a paste of ginger and garlic. In Manipur, the over twenty-nine tribes have their own distinct styles of cooking, each marked by slight variations.

Some tribes like the Hmars of Manipur and the Garos of Meghalaya are known for their love of chillies, and tangal or indigenous soda, an alkaline liquid. Tangal meh (a dish of green leafy vegetables, sometimes seasoned with fermented fish or sun-dried meat for flavour), is one of their favourite dishes.

The Tangkhul Nagas of Manipur are so fond of pork that they have a special earthen pot called *hampai* to cook it in. It imparts a unique flavour unlike an ordinary earthen pot. They are made out of rocks mixed with clay and stone, found about ten kilometres away from the village of Longpi Kajui in Ukhrul, in the Tanghul district of Manipur. They are not made on the wheel, but are moulded by hand. It takes about two hours to complete a piece, and about three days to dry. (One can buy a hampai in Dilli Haat, New Delhi, during the annual North-Eastern craft festival.)

Potato is used as a thickening ingredient in most dishes. In Assam, unripe papaya is used to enhance the flavour of most non-vegetarian dishes. Basic herbs like ginger and garlic are crushed and added at the end of the cooking process. Even when turmeric is used, fresh turmeric is dug out from kitchen gardens, ground and then used. Except for the Meiteis, who rustle up a delicious fish curry using oil and spices, and the Asomiyas who relish a peppery flavour in their favourite fish curry, even non-vegetarian dishes are rarely cooked with oil or spices.

Most of the hill tribes are great meat eaters. Pigs and cows are reared at home for consumption, so pork and beef are popular, unlike mutton (as goats are not reared). However, among Muslims, mutton is much sought after and most restaurants in towns serve it.

Sometimes fat is extracted from pork (by cooking it over low heat till the fat oozes out) and used for cooking. Pork or chicken cooked with tender bamboo shoot is very popular amongst the hill tribes. Chilli powder, ginger and garlic are added for colour and flavour. This is relished with rice. The importance of bamboo shoot can hardly be exaggerated in the North-Eastern diet. It is a widely used ingredient even by the Mizos, Arunachalis and the people of Tripura.

To make sure they never run out of meat, almost every kitchen in the North-East stocks dry meat. The meat is cut into chunks, salted, threaded on to skewers and smoked over kitchen fires or placed in the sun to dry out. In a modern kitchen, the meat can be placed on a low grill till it is dry.

Just as South Indians use coconut for flavouring, the North-East has its own indigenously developed ingredients. Fermented fish and soya bean, known in different regions by different names, are popular flavouring agents. For instance, when the Manipuris prepare ironba, a popular vegetable chutney, a pinch of fermented fish is added for that special flavour. In the same way, when the Nagas prepare akhuni chutney made with chillies, they add fermented soya beans to it.

Green leafy vegetables are never cut with a knife. They are toned or shredded by hand as it is believed that a knife spoils the taste of the food. Also, while boiling vegetables, the pan is not covered; this is done in order to retain the natural colours of the food. Sometimes, vegetables are cooked al dente (cooked so as to be still firm when bitten), which adds to the flavour and nutrient value.

A typical kitchen of the hill tribes in the North-East is spacious. In olden days, people entertained their guests in the kitchen. Everyone sat round the fire, sipping a drink, while the hosts were engaged in their household work. The kitchen was an important place, for it was here that suitors were entertained by young women while they busied themselves with cooking.

Unlike the hill tribes, the Meiteis guard their kitchen like a temple. In the olden days, no guests were entertained in the kitchen as it was believed that that would pollute the atmosphere. The Meiteis did not even allow a family member to enter the kitchen unless he or she had taken a bath.

Above the fireplace of the hill tribes' kitchens are rows of skewers of grilled meat kept for drying. If meat is left over after a feast, they continue the feasting on the next morning till the last piece disappears.

The kitchen is undoubtedly the domain of every North-Eastern woman, but it's not uncommon to see men in the kitchen. In fact, during Christmas and other social festivals, when there are community feasts, it is the men who take over from the women, as their physical strength comes in handy while lifting heavy pots and firewood.

Ideally, every woman is expected to know how to cook. It enhances her qualifications and marriage prospects. Though there are no hard and fast rules about a woman's skill in the kitchen, certain tribes, like the Bodos of Assam, used to attach such importance to this that a woman who did not know how to cook would be unable to find a life partner and considered a social embarrassment. Of course, things are slowly changing and it is not such a hard and fast rule anymore.

Among the Hindus of the Meitei community, the Brahmins or Bamons, as they are locally called, are culinary experts who are traditionally ordained to cook and are hired during special religious or social occasions to prepare the feasts.

In the twelfth century, the Ahoms or Thais of the Shan tribes entered Assam from upper Burma and crossed the Irrawady river to conquer the territory. At the same time, the Mughals conquered India from the west. After reaching the Brahmaputra, the Ahoms started occupying the areas inhabited by the indigenous Bodo tribes and conquered a major part of Assam, which they ruled for 600 years, during which time they also influenced the cuisine of the area in terms of flavour and style of cooking.

The underplay of spices, the use of fermented products, the liberal use of aromatic and fresh herbs and the drying and smoking of meat to preserve it are some examples of this influence. Dishes are seasoned with ingredients belonging to the onion family (such as shallots and green onion), garlic, and the ginger family, including turmeric. The techniques of steaming food and Chinese wok-cooking, in which chopped food is fried, braised, or stewed are also used here.

The use of fermented fish and soya bean among the hill tribes like the Nagas, Mizos, and Khasis resembles the use of fermented seafood that is prepared by the action of microorganisms which chemically change its flavour and appearance in Korean cuisine, and the different varieties of fish and pungent shrimp sauces used in Thai cuisine.

A North-Eastern meal is quick to cook and does not involve elaborate preparations. It is served with all dishes placed on the table at the time, rather than in courses. The dessert, of course, comes at the end of the meal, but this is not served daily, it is mainly served during special feasts.

Wedding ceremonies and religious functions are the best occasions to sample traditional dishes. Most weddings, regardless of tribe or religion, are times for feasting. At Christian weddings among the tribes, it is almost customary to serve as many non-vegetarian dishes as possible.

When it comes to sweets, the people of the North-East cannot match their counterparts from the rest of India. They do not necessarily round off their meals with dessert. While they may enjoy sweets, they prefer the natural flavour of fruits. Almost every home owns a guava or a mango tree, so fruits are seldom purchased at the market. Seasonal fruits such as papayas, pineapples, guavas, mangos, peaches, jackfruits and pomegranates usually complete their meals. In many states, seasonal fruits are made into syrups and reserves, and many bottles have found their way to the local shops. Often, the locally manufactured squashes are preferred to the well-known branded ones, purely due to the natural flavour they contain.

With rice taking the centre stage in the meal, and the abundant fresh vegetables and fruit, supplemented by meat or fish, North-East cooking is high on nutritional value, less on calories, and is actually a high-fibre diet. Experts correlate this diet with the low rate of colon cancer in the people of this region. The freshness of the ingredients and daily cooking results in more nutrients being retained in the food, compared to processed or preheated food.

A North-Eastern meal is always balanced, and for every spicy dish there is a bland one. Among the hill tribes, no meal is complete without plain boiled vegetables known by different names (antui, champhut, etc.) to go with the more spicy dishes. It is the soup of these boiled vegetables that gives the tribesmen the strength to climb the lofty mountains and walk the miles to their fields.

Every tribe in the North-East has its own distinct characteristics with regard to language, dress, festival and culture, and all this is in turn reflected in their cuisine.

On the whole, North-Eastern delicacies are simple to the point of being bland and are cooked without oil or too many spices. Chillies are used in abundance in most dishes, and ginger and garlic are the favourite spices.

In this age of health freaks and diet watchers, the answer to most problems is a low-calorie diet, which is what North-Eastern cuisine is all about.

Steaming plays an important role in North-Eastern cuisine. If you don't have a steamer, place the food to be steamed in a greased pan and place it on a stand in a larger pan with boiling water standing halfway up the sides of the small pan. Cover the large pan with a tight-fitting lid and steam over high heat, replenishing the water with boiling water as needed.

Often, Tibetan or Chinese momos have been associated with North-Eastern food, even though they were never a part of the mainstream menu, except for the Sherdukpen Buddhist sects of Arunachal Pradesh, due to their proximity with China or in Sikkim, where momos and thukpas are part of the rich repertoire, but definitely do not represent the cuisine of the people.

With time, I believe that North-Eastern flavours will only get more popular. More than a decade ago, when the North-East pavilions first experimented with their traditional recipes at Dilli Haat, there were hardly any takers, with the exception of the momos. Today, the mushrooming of speciality North-Eastern restaurants in metros and food festivals featuring North-Eastern cuisine is testimony to the evolution of the Indian palette, indicating that food from the eight states will have a bigger share in the market.

North-Eastern cuisine is just waiting to be discovered and this book is a step in that direction. It is an attempt to introduce the flavours of the region to the rest of the country and add to the culinary richness of Indian cuisine.

SPECIALITY INGREDIENTS

The North-East states use a number of ingredients that are unique to their cuisine. These are mainly herbs and vegetables that grow in the jungles of the area and due to the isolation of these states from the rest of India, many of them are not readily available outside the states. Some items are available in the larger markets of the metropolitan cities.

Akhuni (Fermented Soya Beans)
There are two types of fermented soya beans. One is made with fresh beans which is more pungent and has a sharp smell and the other is made from dried beans, which is milder. Until you have acquired a taste for the pungent one, use dry beans to prepare it.

To make akhuni:
- Wash 1 kg soya beans and cook under pressure with 1 litre of water for about 2 hours. It should be very, very soft. Strain and discard liquid.
- Wash strained beans in cold water and drain well.
- Wrap 2 tbsp of beans in banana leaves to make small parcels. Place parcels in an airtight container for 3–4 days in summer and about 5 days in winter.

Angoithi Seeds
These are jungle chillies; use black pepper as a substitute.

Bamboo Mushrooms
They grow on the barks of trees in the jungles of the North-East. They are black in colour, but unlike other black mushrooms, bamboo mushrooms have a velvety texture. However, black mushrooms can be used in their place.

Bamboo Shoot
Bamboo shoot is an essential ingredient of North-Eastern cuisine and is now available in the markets of many large cities across the country.

In case fresh bamboo shoot is not available you can use the canned ones.

Bamboo Shoot—Fermented
To prepare fermented bamboo shoot, wash bamboo shoot and cut into 1" pieces. Place in a large airtight container for 2 weeks without touching them.

Wash well in lukewarm water, drain and use.

Fermented Fish
Fermented fish is prepared locally by many tribes of the North-East. The Tripuris and Meiteis are particularly fond of adding this to their preparations to add zing to the dish.

Fish, preferably river fish is washed and packed into an airtight container—as much as can be pressed in. It is then left untouched in a corner of the house for a week. By then it develops a certain stage of pungency and the process of fermentation is complete.

Indigenous Soda
Many tribes of the North-East, like the Hmars of Manipur, Garos of Meghalaya and Bodos of Assam use an indigenously prepared alkaline liquid which they call soda.

It is made by burning the dried trunk of a banana tree and

mixing the ashes with water in a container. A hole is made in the container and the alkaline liquid that percolates through is called soda.

Sodium bicarbonate can be used as a substitute, but the taste is not the same.

Lengmaser
This herb is found in the jungles of Manipur, Mizoram and Nagaland. The flower of the plant is used, and it can give the blandest dish a fresh flavour and aroma. It belongs to the tulsi family. It grows as a shrub and many people of the North-East cultivate it in their kitchen gardens. It is a seasonal plant, and during the season the fresh flowers are used. They are also dried and stored for future use when the plant is not flowering.

Mizo Anthur
This is a herb found only in Mizoram and Manipur; use mustard leaves as a substitute.

Parkia
The fruit of the parkia tree, which is found almost all over the North-East is used as a herb. It is long, light green in colour and has a strong smell. It is called by different names by the different tribes. In Manipur the Paites call it zongtah, Meiteis call it youngchak while the Mizos call it zongtrah. It is called satau in Thai.

Since it is a huge tree, not many people can pluck the fruit. There are legends that maintain that if anyone attempting to pluck the fruit falls off the tree he gets possessed by an evil spirit. In fact in the olden days, there were special experts whose skill was reserved only for plucking parkia fruit.

There is no real substitute for this.

Raja Chillies
Fiery hot, round, red chillies, the size of gooseberries, they are found only in the jungles of Nagaland, Manipur and Mizoram. You can use any hot chillies in their place.

Repchi
These are small, green, round chillies, smaller than a green pea. They are found in the jungles of Nagaland and called repchi by the Ao tribe. They are often dried and preserved like any other chilli. When the Ao make their chutneys, a little repchi is always added, and this ensures that the meal will be good.

Sticky Rice
Sticky rice is a special variety of fat-grained rice used by the people of the North-East. It is called bera saul in Assamese. The grains stick together when the rice is cooked and it is relished by the people there.

Sun-dried Fish
Sun-dried fish from the North-East is available in unbranded packets, at INA market in Delhi, but any sun-dried river fish can be used in its place.

Tangmo
A sour powder made from the bark of a tree whose botanical name is *Rhuft semieliata*, it is not available outside the North-East. Use lime juice in its place.

Tangmo is also used by the Ao tribe while dying cloth with indigo, as it helps to make the colour fast.

TABLE OF MEASURES

The cup measure used in this book is a 200 ml cup

1 tsp = 5 ml
1 tbsp = 3 tsp
A pinch = $1/8$ tsp (literally a pinch)

All spoon measures are level

ARUNACHAL PRADESH

Feasts from the Tribal Kitchen

The simplicity of the Arunachalis is reflected in their food, which is easy and quick to prepare. All you need is a vegetable of your choice and some home-grown ginger for flavouring; no spices for colouring, and no oil to camouflage the look. With little or no embellishments, the food preserves its natural freshness. Arunachalis appreciate good food and often make an occasion out of their meal. They love to sip their opo (rice beer), no matter what hour of the day, and they must never run short of it. They begin their day early and start it with opo. The main ingredient is rice which is parboiled, mixed with yeast and dried in the sun for six hours. It is then mixed with water and kept undisturbed for two to three days to ferment, after which it is distilled.

After they have had their share of the heady liquid, they are ready to face the day. The men take some opo in a bottle to the fields where they sip it occasionally whenever they are tired. It serves as a stimulant and an energizer that keeps them alert through the day.

Opo can be preserved for days and sometimes for weeks. There is no household that lacks opo. It is the first thing served to visitors and it is impolite to refuse. Whether it is a marriage ceremony or religious one, no social function is complete without opo.

Rice is the staple diet for the twenty-six tribes and approximately two hundred sub-tribes of Arunachal Pradesh. They are non-vegetarians who rear domestic animals like pigs, mithun (a type of buffalo) and chicken for their consumption. They fatten these animals through the year and slaughter them on special occasions. They do not rear goats but most restaurants in towns serve goat's meat.

The Buddhist Monpa and Sherdukpa tribes are more inclined towards Chinese food, rather than the typical Arunachali food. While rice also forms a part of their staple diet, they favour momos, chowmein and thukpa. Momos are usually stuffed with minced pork, and sometimes mustard greens and an assortment of other green vegetables.

Chillies and ginger are the most useful flavourings. In order to make the aroma of ginger linger on, it is added after the dish is removed from heat; the pot is covered immediately and left for a few minutes for the aroma to develop. Sometimes some of the herbs found in the jungles are also added. In the villages, due to non-availability of spices, the food is on the bland side. The Idumishmi tribe, inhabitants of Roing, for example, have mainly boiled food. However, in towns like Itanagar, spices are increasingly getting popular. Even here, they are sparingly used. Bamboo shoot remains an important flavouring and enhancing ingredient. The Adi tribe, for example, prepares ekung, a simple dish of bamboo shoot and chillies.

At marriages, most tribes serve chicken and pork. Even on special occasions, they do not use oil. Amin oying, a chicken stew, for example, is made by boiling chicken in a minimum of water with ingredients like ginger and chillies while arek is made with fresh pork and bamboo shoot. Sometimes broken rice is added to a dish to thicken the gravy.

Just as each tribe differs in terms of dress, so too their style of cooking. Today in Itanagar, fried items are becoming increasingly popular. Deep-fried pork or chicken has become a part of the daily menu. Fish is not part of the regular diet due to its scarcity, but they can walk miles into the jungle for fishing. They explode bombs in the river, and when the dead fish float on the surface, they collect them.

The Adi tribe is fond of smoked meat. In most Adi kitchens, there are rows of skewers with meat kept over the fireplace for smoking and drying. Among the Idumishmi tribe, when an animal is killed it is divided equally between all the village households, so there is usually not enough meat left to dry and preserve. This does not happen with the Adi tribe, so each family has enough meat stored for days when fresh meat is not available.

Since the agricultural produce of Arunachal Pradesh consist of rice, maize, millet and potatoes, their diet revolves around these items. Even the preparation of dishes during festivals is not really different from their daily cooking. The only difference, perhaps, is in the quantity.

Some Buddhist tribes like the Sherdukpas, Khamptis and Khamiyangs do not eat beef which is considered a delicacy among other tribes. Their faith plays an important role in dictating what they eat. Mutton is taboo for the Buddhists, who are settled in West Kameng, Tawang, and the plains of Lohit and Tirap districts. Most of them are followers of Donyi-Polo. Lamaistic Buddhists such as the Monpas, Sherdukpas, Membas and Khambas celebrate the Losar festival—a festival of joy and rejoicing, which marks the Tibetan New Year. It is their most important festival and lasts for fifteen days around January/February.

Sangken is the most important festival of the Khamptis, Khamiyangs and Singphos. It lasts for three days in the middle of April as a spring festival. During this festival, the monks and villagers pour water on the image of Lord Buddha and sprinkle water on each other with great fun and merriment.

Among the Adis, Solung is one of the most popular and colourful festivals celebrated during July/August. The festival lasts for seven days. It is connected with agricultural activities and has a socio-economic significance.

The major festival of the Nishis is Nyokum which is observed to propitiate the gods for a rich harvest. It falls in the month of August. This festival is marked with song and dance, and people offer prayers to the deities for a good harvest, good health and for the vitality of domesticated animals. The Nishis also celebrate the Longteyalu festival.

The most important festival of the Mijis is Khan which is held in February/March. It is a great occasion for merriment, with song and dance.

The Apatanis of Subansiri district observe the Dree festival to propitiate deities for a bumper crop and prosperity. Song and dance is a major part of the festival. It is held in July and lasts for three days.

To the people of Arunachal Pradesh, festivals are a time to eat and make merry. It's a time to sit back and share a meal with loved ones.

OYING
VEGETABLE STEW

Serves: 3

1 kg mixture of mustard leaves, cabbage, French beans and potatoes
2–3 green chillies, chopped
1 tsp salt
1 tsp ginger paste

- Wash vegetables. Tear mustard and cabbage leaves in half by hand.
- Trim beans and break in half.
- Peel and cut potatoes into ½" cubes.
- Place 2½ cups water in a pan and bring to boil over high heat.
- Add vegetables and cook till tender.
- Stir in green chillies and salt.
- Heat through if necessary before serving, mix in ginger, cover pan and leave for 5 minutes.
- Serve with steamed rice.

THUKPA
VEGETABLE STEW WITH NOODLES

Serves: 2

500 gms noodles
5 cups stock (vegetable, chicken or pork)
2 cups prepared and chopped mixed vegetables (beans, cabbage, carrots, etc.)
2 tsp salt

Garnish:
2 tbsp chopped fresh coriander leaves

- Cook noodles in a large pan, with plenty of boiling salted water to which a few drops of oil are added, till just tender (al dente—with a bite).
- Drain and run cold water over noodles for 5 minutes.
- Drain again.
- Heat stock in a pan and add vegetables.
- Stir well and add noodles.
- Simmer over moderate heat till vegetables are tender.
- Mix in salt, garnish with coriander leaves and serve.

> **VARIATION:**
> 2 cups shredded chicken can be added with the vegetables.

EKUNG

TENDER BAMBOO SHOOT WITH CHILLIES

Serves: 5

500 gms bamboo shoot (baans ki kalli)
4 green chillies, ground to a paste
1½ tsp salt

- Wash bamboo shoot and drain thoroughly. Cut into thin, 1" long slices.
- Combine green chillies with salt and mix with bamboo shoot.
- Place mixture in a pan over moderate heat and stir and cook for about 10 minutes.
- The mixture should be a little moist.
- Serve as a side dish.

ASIN PUINAM
FISH IN BAMBOO HOLLOW

Serves: 5

This is a popular item prepared during picnics or in the jungles while hunting.

500 gms small fresh river fish
2½ cups rice
1 tsp ginger paste
3 green chillies, chopped
1 tsp salt
2 bamboo hollows, 3" in diameter and 5" long

- Clean fish and cut into suitable sized pieces if large.
- Wash fish and drain thoroughly.
- Wash rice and drain well.
- Combine all ingredients and place in bamboo hollows.
- Seal mouth of bamboos with foil to make them airtight.
- Place bamboos over a charcoal fire and cook for about 30 minutes. Rotate bamboos from time to time to cook evenly.
- Serve in the bamboos.

> **NOTE:**
> The mixture can be wrapped in thick layers of foil and baked in an oven preheated to 105ºC/225ºF for 15 minutes.

ILI
PORK STEW WITH GINGER

Serves: 5

1 kg pork
1 cup broken rice
3" piece ginger, chopped 1 tsp red chilli powder
1 tsp salt

- Wash pork, drain and cut into 2" pieces.
- Wash rice, drain and mix with pork.
- Place 1 litre water in a pan and bring to boil over high heat.
- Add pork and rice, and bring to boil again, stirring constantly.
- Lower heat, simmer for 2 minutes and add remaining ingredients.
- Cover pan and cook for 30 minutes, till pork is tender and gravy thickens.
- Serve with steamed rice.

AREK

PORK STEW WITH BAMBOO SHOOT

Serves: 4

1 kg pork
3 tsp chopped bamboo shoot (baans ki kalli)
1 tsp chopped ginger
1 tsp chopped garlic
1 medium-sized tomato, quartered
3–4 green chillies, chopped
1 tsp salt

- Wash pork, drain and cut into 1" pieces.
- Place pork in a pan over high heat with enough water to cover. Just before it starts to boil, drain water.
- Return pork to pan, add fresh water to cover and bring to boil.
- Mix in remaining ingredients, cover pan, lower heat and simmer for 30 minutes, till pork is tender.
- Serve with steamed rice.

LUKTAR

DRIED PORK AND BAMBOO SHOOT PICKLE

Makes: 750 gms

500 gms dried pork
1 cup dried bamboo shoot (baans ki kalli)
Bamboo or metal skewers
3 tsp red chilli powder
1½ tsp salt

- Cut pork into 1" pieces and bamboo shoot into ½" pieces.
- Thread pork onto skewers and roast over a charcoal fire for 15–20 minutes till it turns reddish and tender.
- Keep rotating skewers to ensure even cooking.
- Allow to cool and shred.
- Combine all ingredients, mix well and store in an airtight jar.
- It can be stored for months.

GORU ADIN
STIR-FRIED BEEF

Serves: 6

1 kg beef
3 tbsp oil
6 green chillies, chopped
1 heaped tsp ginger paste
3 tsp black pepper powder
1½ tsp salt

- Wash beef, drain thoroughly and cut into 2" pieces.
- Heat oil in a kadhai or wok, add green chillies and stir-fry for a few moments.
- Add beef and stir-fry till brown.
- Cover kadhai or wok and cook over low heat for 1 hour till tender.
- Keep checking and stirring occasionally to ensure that it does not stick to base of kadhai. If it gets too dry sprinkle in some water.
- Stir in remaining ingredients and continue stirring over low heat for another 5–10 minutes.

> **NOTE:**
> This is served in small portions as a side dish.

ASO ADIN
MUTTON STEW WITH GINGER

Serves: 5

This dish has a delicious ginger tang.

**1 kg mutton
1 heaped tsp ginger paste
5 green chillies, chopped
2 tsp salt**

- Wash mutton, drain and cut into 2" pieces.
- Place 3 cups water in a pan and bring to boil over high heat.
- Add mutton and continue boiling for 5 minutes.
- Stir in remaining ingredients, cover pan and simmer till mutton is tender and gravy thickens.
- Serve with steamed rice.

CHOW-CHOW

NOODLES WITH MEAT AND VEGETABLES

Serves: 3

300 gms cooked boneless beef, pork, chicken or mutton
 tbsp oil
2 medium-sized tomatoes, chopped
2 medium-sized onions, chopped
½ medium-sized cabbage, chopped
500 gms noodles
2 tsp salt

Garnish:
1 tbsp chopped fresh coriander leaves

- Shred meat and set aside.
- Heat oil in a kadhai or wok. Add vegetables and stir-fry for 5 minutes.
- Add meat and continue to stir-fry for a further 10 minutes.
- Cook noodles in a large pan, with plenty of boiling salted water to which a few drops of oil are added, till just tender (al dente—with a bite).
- Drain and run cold water over noodles for 5 minutes.
- Drain again.
- Add noodles and salt to kadhai, heat through, garnish with coriander leaves and serve with any sauce of your choice.

AMIN OYING
CHICKEN STEW

Serves: 5

1 kg chicken
1 tsp chopped ginger
3 green chillies, chopped
1½ tsp salt
½ cup broken rice

- Cut chicken into 2" pieces and wash.
- Place chicken in a pan with 1 litre water and bring to boil over high heat. Continue boiling for 5 minutes.
- Mix in ginger, green chillies and salt.
- Wash rice and stir it in.
- Bring to boil, lower heat and simmer for about 15 minutes, stirring occasionally, till chicken and rice are cooked and gravy thickens.

> **NOTE:**
> Amin oying is usually served in small bowls made of banana leaves before an opo (rice beer) is served.

ETOH

CHICKEN STEW WITH GINGER

Serves: 4

**2 kg chicken
3" piece ginger, chopped
1 tsp red chilli powder
1½ tsp salt**

- Clean chicken, cut into medium-sized pieces and wash.
- Place 1 litre water in a pan and bring to boil over high heat.
- Add chicken and cook for 5 minutes.
- Mix in remaining ingredients and cook, stirring occasionally till chicken is tender.
- Ensure that there is enough water to cover the chicken at all times. There should be enough gravy for each serving.
- Serve with steamed rice.

RONGPU TAKENG
EGG CHUTNEY

Serves: 3

5 eggs, hard-boiled
1 tsp ginger paste
1 tsp salt

- Peel and mash eggs to a smooth paste.
- Mix in ginger and salt.

NOTE:
It is usually served with opo (rice beer).

MOMOS

Makes: about 15 momos

4 cups plain flour (maida)
500 gms mince (beef, pork or chicken)
1 cup onion paste
1 tsp salt

- Sift flour into a bowl and knead to a soft, fine dough with 2–3 cups of water.
- Combine mince, onions and salt, and mix well.
- Pinch off egg-sized balls of dough and roll into balls.
- Flatten a ball in your palm and place 1 tbsp filling in the centre. Fold over sides to shape into a triangle or round, and press edges firmly to seal.
- Make remaining momos in the same way.
- Grease the upper container of a steamer, place momos in it and steam for 10 minutes.
- Serve with a chutney.

ETHING

RICE CAKE STEAMED IN BANANA LEAVES

Makes: about 10 cakes

500 gms rice
2 banana leaves

- Grind rice to a fine powder.
- Clean banana leaves with a damp cloth on both sides.
- Dry and pass over a live flame to make them pliable, taking care not to burn the leaves. Cut banana leaves into 8" squares.
- Sift rice powder into a bowl, gradually add 2 cups water and knead to a soft dough.
- Place about ½ cup dough in the centre of each banana leaf square and fold to make parcels. Tie with cotton string to secure parcels.
- Steam for 20 minutes.
- Serve with tea or opo (rice beer).

TS-JA
TEA WITH YAK'S MILK

Serves: 2

Like the Bhutanis, the Arunachalis love salted tea.

1 cup yak's milk or 1 tsp salt-free butter
½ tsp salt
1 tsp tea leaves

- Place 2 cups water in a pan and bring to boil.
- Add yak's milk or butter and salt.
- Bring to boil again and add tea leaves.
- Cover pan, remove from heat and leave to infuse for 5 minutes.
- Strain tea and serve.

ASSAM

Meals from the Banks of the Brahmaputra

Food habits in Assam are as diverse as the languages spoken there. The Bodos, who are the indigenous tribe, relish sobai jwng oma vedor, their traditional dish of pork and husked black beans (urad dal) cooked without oil or spices. They rustle up this dish whenever they want a special meal. For the majority Asomiya community, there is no substitute to masor jhol, a fish curry prepared in a minimum of oil and spices. Unlike the Asomiyas who restrict themselves to fresh fish, the Bodos are dependent on fermented fish called napham (pronounced napam), the aroma of which whets the appetite. Napham is also an essential ingredient of napham bathun, a mouth-watering, fiery chutney.

To compliment their meals, the Bodos and other tribes like the Karbi, Mishing and Rabha drink zou, a kind of rice beer. It keeps their bodies active and warm. It is brewed at home and every home has a stock of zou which they offer their guests in place of tea.

The Assamese on the whole are rice eaters. The main difference between the majority Asomiyas and the other tribes, is the latter's preference for pork, zou and sun-dried and fermented fish. Since the Asomiyas had long settled along the banks of the Brahmaputra, fresh fish was always available, so there was no need to dry it and their preference for fresh fish is more due to habit than any religious or cultural belief. However, pork is considered impure and they abstain from it due to social reservations.

The use of lemon grass, coconut milk, chilli paste and bamboo shoot in the preparation of some of the Assamese dishes are a part of the Thai influence.

Every region boasts its own food speciality, but on the whole, Assamese food is known for its simplicity. Unlike most of the hill tribes of the North-East, they may use oil but this is kept to the minimum. They are health-conscious and use spices only when they prepare non-vegetarian dishes. For instance, they prepare mansha jhol, a mutton curry, with pepper. Sometimes unripe papaya is added for thickening the gravy and mellowing the flavour. The generous use of mustard seeds in their fish curries is an influence of the Bengalis who have settled in large numbers in Assam, but they do not use as much as the Bengalis and they prefer green chillies to the red ones. Other than their use of mustard seeds, they do not share a common culinary identity, as is often mistakenly thought.

The Assamese also use souring agents in some of their dishes, but unlike the South Indians, they use lime and tomato and not tamarind.

While mutton is a popular non-vegetarian item, chicken, fish, duck and pigeon are equally popular. In some parts of Assam like Lakhimpur district, the villagers rear ducks and serve it at special occasions.

Residents of Dibrugarh in upper Assam eat steamed rice with dal and khar (lightly boiled vegetables). The dal is usually fried in a little oil after lightly browning some onions. Here, the food is less spicy compared to other parts of Assam. The use of fenugreek seeds for flavour is quite common, but in the absence of fenugreek they use mustard seeds. They relish duck with the same weakness as the residents of other parts of Assam. Unlike the enterprising villagers of Lakhimpur district, residents of Dibrugarh do not rear ducks at home but prefer to buy them from the market. Chicken and mutton too are purchased from local butcher shops.

As you move down to lower Assam—Kamrup, Nalbari, Barbeta, Bongaigaon, Kukhreja, Golpara and Dhuburi—the taste gets spicier and when they prepare khar, they often add fish to it. There is less emphasis on tenga (sourness) and a generous use of coconut in the dishes. Since there are abundant coconut trees in lower Assam, it is used in many dishes, including nariyal ka ladoo (coconut sweet made with grated fresh coconut and hot ghee). Nearly every household makes its own typical nariyal ka ladoo.

In Majuli Island, the world's largest river island, the indigenous Mishing and Deori tribes who are the main residents of the island also drink zou. There is hardly any oil or basic spices like turmeric in their cooking. Vegetables and meat boiled in water and seasoned with herbs found on the island constitute their simple diet. Only when they prepare pork do they use a hint of spices with rice powder added to thicken the gravy.

Central Assam has more variety in its food as it has accommodated different faiths that have coexisted there for years. Guwahati, for example, reflects a more cosmopolitan spirit that is prominent even in their food, and it would be a hard task to find a restaurant here that serves a typical Asomiya dish. Instead, what you see are restaurants catering to food from the different communities of neighbouring states. The only constant trend is the absence of too many spices, with ginger and garlic being the predominant ones. Often, they prefer deep-fried items, which are not popular in most parts of Assam and they like their mutton well-spiced and finger-licking. This is the influence of the younger generations of Assamese who now intermingle with different communities and act as agents in promoting cultural exchanges, so that slowly the cuisine too is undergoing changes. While a South Indian may not prepare zou, an Asomiya housewife can spend the afternoon perfecting her dosa or idli. Despite all these new influences, their staple food still consists of dal, which is prepared only with salt, and fish and chicken.

Coconut ladoo is also still popular. At marriages, they serve chera patha doi—a sweet made from curd, jaggery and instant rice called komal saul. They also eat poori-subji and sweets like petha.

Bodos serve non-vegetarian food on all occasions and from ancient times have preserved meat to last them a year. Large quantities of meat—mainly pork—is skewered, salted and smoked over a fire or dried in the sun. One or two pieces of this meat is eaten during a meal, or mixed into a dish to enhance its flavour.

The kitchen has always been the domain of the women in Bodo society. Knowing how to cook is considered a necessity and a woman who can't cook finds it difficult to find a husband, no matter how rich she may be.

The Bodos, being the indigenous people of the land, are quite different, even in the food they eat, from the rest of the Indo-Aryans of Assam. They also use the indigenous soda. One of the most important Bodo dishes is sobai wangkhrai, a chicken and black bean (urad dal) preparation. This is a symbolic dish served during special occasions like Rongali which falls in April. It is a seven-day festival like the Rongali Bihu of the Assamese and is linked to the start of the new agricultural season. It is marked by feasting and dance. They drink zou or rice beer with well-prepared meat. Then, they march in groups to the fields to get the blessings of the almighty. They worship sijou bijang, a cactus plant, which is the symbol of their god. Every Bodo home has a sijou bijang planted in the courtyard facing the east, as they believe the god they worship dwells in the east.

During Bodo weddings, the surrounding villagers are invited to bless the newly married couple. The bride-to-be, with the help of another lady of the village, prepares sobai wangkhrai which is served to the guests, after which the marriage rituals are performed. This is meant to be a test of the new bride's culinary skills. If the dish is tasty, she will have impressed the villagers, otherwise the household will be criticized and even mocked. When sobai wangkhrai is prepared for a wedding, no turmeric or colouring essence is added.

ALU PITIKA
SPICY MASHED POTATOES

Serves: 4

2 medium-sized potatoes
1 tsp mustard oil
1 medium-sized onion, chopped
2 green chillies, chopped
½ tsp salt

Garnish:
1 tbsp chopped fresh coriander leaves

- Boil potatoes, peel and mash.
- Combine all ingredients except garnish and mix well.
- Garnish with coriander leaves and serve as a side dish at lunch or dinner.

KOSU HAJOR
SOUR COLOCASIA LEAF CURRY

Serves: 4

This is one of the favourite dishes of the Assamese.

500 gms colocasia leaves with tender stems (arvi patta)
2 tbsp mustard oil
1 medium-sized onion, finely chopped
1 tsp ginger paste
1 tsp garlic paste
½ tbsp coriander powder
½ tbsp black pepper powder
½ tbsp cumin powder
½ tbsp turmeric powder
1 tsp salt
2 tsp lime juice

- Wash colocasia leaves and tear by hand.
- Place leaves in a pan with water to cover and cook for 15–20 minutes, till tender. Drain and set aside.
- Heat oil in a kadhai or wok, add onion and fry till golden brown.
- Mix in ginger, garlic and spice powders, and fry for a few minutes.
- Stir in colocasia leaves and salt, and continue frying for a few minutes, stirring constantly.
- Add 2½ cups water and boil for 10 minutes.
- Mix in lime juice and continue boiling till gravy thickens.
- Serve with steamed rice.

MATI DAL
BLACK BEANS WITH PUMPKIN

Serves: 4–5

250 gms whole black beans (sabut urad)
250 gms white pumpkin (doodhiya)
¼ tsp turmeric powder
1 tbsp mustard oil
2 large onions, chopped
10 cloves garlic, chopped
1 tsp ginger paste

- Wash beans and soak in water for 2 hours.
- Wash, peel and clean pumpkin, and cut into large pieces.
- Place beans, pumpkin, turmeric and 1 litre water in a pressure cooker and cook under pressure for 20 minutes.
- Heat oil in a kadhai or wok, add onions and garlic, and fry till onions turn golden brown.
- Pour contents of pressure cooker into kadhai and mix well.
- Heat through if necessary before serving, mix in ginger, cover pan and simmer for 5 minutes.

> **NOTE:**
> This dish is normally served at lunch as it is very heavy.

KHAR—I

BLACK BEANS WITH UNRIPE PAPAYA

Serves: 5

200 gms whole black beans (sabut urad)
1 tsp + 1 tsp mustard oil
1 tsp fenugreek seeds (methi)
2 cups peeled, grated unripe papaya
1 tsp salt
½ tsp sugar
2 drops indigenous soda or ½ tsp sodium bicarbonate
1 tsp ginger paste

- Wash beans and place in a pan with 2½ cups water.
- Bring to boil, and boil for 10 minutes. Drain and set aside.
- Heat 1 tsp oil in a kadhai or wok and add fenugreek seeds. When they start sputtering, add beans and papaya, and fry for about 10 minutes, stirring constantly.
- Stir in salt, sugar, soda or sodium bicarbonate and 2½ cups water, and cook stirring occasionally till papaya and beans are tender and gravy thickens.
- Remove from heat and stir in ginger and 1 tsp oil.
- Serve with steamed rice.

KHAR—II

BOTTLEGOURD WITH FISH

Serves: 5

This dish is popular in the lower Assam region.

500 gms bottlegourd (lauki)
4 tsp oil
2 bay leaves (tej patta)
4 green chillies, slit
2 cloves garlic, finely chopped
4 drops indigenous soda or 1 tsp sodium bicarbonate
250 gms small fish, cleaned, washed and fried till golden brown
2 tsp salt

Garnish:
1 tbsp chopped fresh coriander leaves

- Peel bottlegourd, clean, wash and chop fine.
- Heat oil in a pan, add bay leaves, green chillies and garlic, and fry, stirring constantly, for 2 minutes.
- Add bottlegourd and soda or sodium bicarbonate, and continue cooking for a few minutes, stirring frequently to prevent burning.
- Pour in 2½ cups water, cover pan, lower heat and simmer for 20 minutes, stirring occasionally.
- Stir in fish and salt, and cook for another 5 minutes.
- Remove from heat, garnish with coriander leaves and serve with steamed rice.

NAPHAM
FISH WITH COLOCASIA LEAVES

Serves: 5

1 kg small fresh river fish
500 gms colocasia leaves (arvi patta)
2 tsp salt
1 bamboo hollow, 3" in diameter and 5" long

- Wash fish, drain and spread out in the sun, covered with a thin muslin cloth for a day to dry completely.
- Wash and clean colocasia leaves and grind coarsely.
- Mix in fish and salt.
- Place mixture into bamboo hollow and press tightly.
- Seal carefully with foil to ensure it is airtight, and set aside for a month, after which it is ready to eat.
- Empty contents into a bowl and serve as a side dish with rice and any other dishes.

> **NOTE:**
> This process of keeping a mixture in a bamboo hollow to mature is called owa hasung. Make sure the bamboo hollow is completely dry

NAPHAM BATHUN
FERMENTED FISH CHUTNEY

Serves: 5

7 dried red or fresh green chillies
3 small fermented fish
2 medium-sized tomatoes, chopped
1 onion, chopped
1 tsp salt

- Heat a tawa or griddle and roast chillies till dark and fragrant. Remove from tawa and set aside.
- Add fish to tawa and roast for 2–3 minutes, till soft.
- Sprinkle over a little water to prevent fish from sticking to tawa.
- Combine all ingredients, mash to a paste and serve.

MAAS PATOTIA
FISH ROASTED IN BANANA LEAVES

Serves: 5

1 kg fish, kept whole (use any fish with a single central bone)
1 tsp mustard oil
3 banana leaves

Marinade:
3 green chillies, finely chopped
1 medium-sized onion, finely chopped
1 tsp mustard seeds, ground
1 tsp salt

- Clean fish, wash and drain thoroughly.
- Combine ingredients for marinade, rub into fish, sprinkle over oil and marinate for 15 minutes.
- Clean banana leaves with a damp cloth on both sides.
- Dry and pass over a live flame to make them pliable, taking care not to burn the leaves. Cut banana leaves into suitable sizes.
- Wrap each fish in banana leaf to form a parcel and tie with string to secure it.
- Place a tawa or griddle over moderate heat and place a fish parcel on it. Roast on both sides till the leaf is burnt and you get the aroma of burnt leaf and cooked fish.
- Cook remaining fish parcels in the same way.
- Undo parcels, place fish in a serving platter and serve with steamed rice.

MAAS-PATOT-DIA
FISH BAKED IN BANANA LEAVES

Serves: 5

500 gms fish fillet
¾ cup oil
½ cup grated fresh coconut
8 dry red chillies, broken into 2 pieces each
2 medium-sized onions, finely chopped
2 cloves garlic, finely chopped
2 stalks lemon grass, chopped
2 eggs, lightly beaten
2 tbsp chopped cashewnuts or almonds
½ cup thick coconut milk
2 tsp salt
¼ tsp black pepper powder
3 banana leaves

- Wash fish, drain thoroughly and mince.
- Heat 2 tbsp oil in a pan, add coconut and fry for 2–3 minutes. Drain and set aside.
- Pour remaining oil into pan and heat through.
- Add red chillies, onions, garlic and lemon grass, and fry till onions turn pale gold.
- Stir in fish, eggs, nuts and reserved coconut, and fry till golden brown.
- Mix in coconut milk, salt and pepper, and simmer till gravy thickens.
- Clean banana leaves with a damp cloth on both sides.
- Dry and pass over a live flame to make them pliable, taking care not to burn the leaves. Cut banana leaves into 8" squares.
- Lightly grease banana leaves and place 1 cup of mixture in the centre of each piece. Wrap to form parcels and secure with toothpicks or string.

- Place on a greased baking tray and bake in an oven preheated to 180ºC/350ºF for 35–40 minutes.
- Unwrap parcels and serve with steamed rice.

NOTES:
You can use foil in place of the banana leaves.
This dish is traditionally cooked directly over a charcoal fire.

VARIATION:
Instead of minced fish, you can use very small fish.

MASOR JHOL—I
FISH CURRY

Serves: 4

1 kg carp (rohu)
2 tbsp oil
2 tsp finely chopped onion
½ tsp ginger paste
½ tsp garlic paste
2 medium-sized potatoes, cut into 1" cubes
1 tsp cumin powder
½ tsp coriander powder
½ tsp turmeric powder
1 kg cauliflower, cut into florets

Marinade:
1 tsp turmeric powder 1 tsp salt

Garnish:
tbsp chopped fresh coriander leaves

- Clean fish, cut into medium-sized pieces, wash and drain thoroughly.
- Combine ingredients for marinade, rub into fish and marinate for 15 minutes.
- Heat oil in a kadhai or wok and lightly fry fish in batches. Drain and set aside.
- Add onion, ginger and garlic to kadhai, and fry, stirring constantly till golden brown.
- Mix in potatoes and 2½ cups water, and bring to boil.
- Sprinkle in spice powders, lower heat and simmer till potatoes are half cooked.
- Add cauliflower and continue simmering till vegetables are tender and gravy thickens.

- Gently mix in fish and simmer for a few minutes longer.
- Garnish with coriander leaves and serve.

> **VARIATION:**
> The fish can also be made with 2 chopped tomatoes, a cup of shelled green peas and 10 finely chopped spinach leaves, instead of potatoes and cauliflower

MASOR JHOL—II
FISH CURRY

Serves: 6

This dish is popular in the lower Assam areas.

500 gms fish fillet or steaks
Oil for deep frying
4 fresh red chillies, broken into 2 pieces
1 large onion, finely chopped
2 cloves garlic, crushed
2 tbsp Thai red curry paste
2 tsp salt
¼ tsp freshly ground black pepper
1½ cups thick coconut milk
2 spring onions, chopped

Garnish:
2 tbsp finely chopped fresh coriander leaves

- Wash fish and drain thoroughly.
- Heat oil in a kadhai or wok till almost smoking. Add fish in batches and deep fry till golden brown. Drain and set aside.
- Remove oil from kadhai leaving only 1 tbsp in it.
- Return kadhai to heat, stir in red chillies, onion and garlic, and fry, stirring constantly for 4–5 minutes.
- Mix in curry paste, salt and pepper, and continue frying, stirring frequently, till oil separates.
- Blend in coconut milk and bring to boil.
- Lower heat and simmer for a few minutes. (Add some water if you want more gravy.)
- Gently mix in spring onions and reserved fish, and simmer for another 10 minutes.

- Remove from heat and transfer curry to a serving dish.
- Garnish with coriander leaves and serve with steamed rice.

NOTE:
Thai red curry paste is available in stores that stock oriental foodstuff.

MASOR TENGA
SOUR FISH
Serves: 5–6

This dish is usually served as the last course of a meal by the Assamese.

500 gms river fish
4 tbsp mustard oil
¼ tsp fenugreek seeds (methi)
½ cup grated bottlegourd (lauki)
½ cup chopped tomatoes
¼ tsp turmeric powder
1 tsp salt
1 tsp lime juice

Marinade:
1 tbsp turmeric powder
1 tbsp salt

Garnish:
1 tbsp chopped fresh coriander leaves

- Clean fish, cut into pieces, wash and drain thoroughly.
- Combine ingredients for marinade, rub into fish and marinate for 10 minutes.
- Rinse fish in fresh water and drain thoroughly.
- Heat oil in a kadhai or wok till smoking, add fish, a few pieces at a time and fry till light brown on both sides. Drain and set aside.
- Lower heat, add fenugreek to kadhai and fry till light brown.
- Stir in bottlegourd and continue frying over low heat for 5 minutes.
- Blend in tomatoes and fry till soft and tender.

- Add turmeric, salt and 2 cups water, and bring to boil.
- Gently add reserved fish, cover pan and simmer for 10 minutes.
- Mix in lime juice and remove from heat.
- Garnish with coriander leaves and serve hot with steamed rice.

OMA BEDOR SAONAI
BARBECUED PORK

Serves: 5

1 kg pork
2 tsp salt Bamboo or metal skewers

- Wash pork, drain thoroughly and cut into 1" pieces.
- Sprinkle over salt and mix thoroughly.
- Thread pork onto skewers and roast over a charcoal fire for 15–30 minutes, turning frequently till golden brown and tender.

OMA EONAI

FRIED PORK

Serves: 5

1 kg pork
2 tbsp oil
1 tbsp ginger paste
1 tbsp garlic paste
1 tbsp onion paste
1 tsp salt

- Wash pork, drain thoroughly and cut into 1" pieces.
- Heat oil in a kadhai or wok, add ginger, garlic and onion, and fry stirring constantly, till golden brown.
- Mix in pork and salt, and fry till brown, stirring frequently.
- Sprinkle in ½ cup water, cover pan and simmer for 30 minutes till tender.

OMA VEDOR GWRAN
SUN-DRIED PORK

This is the ancient method of preserving pork.

1 kg pork

- Wash pork, pat dry and cut into 3" pieces.
- Spread out on trays, cover with a thin muslin cloth and leave in the sun for a week.
- Another traditional method is to thread pork onto skewers and leave it over the fireplace for a week to dry out.
- The pork will stay for a year. It should be placed in the sun from time to time to keep it free from fungus, etc.
- Before serving, heat it gently.

MANSHA JHOL
MUTTON CURRY

Serves: 4

500 gms mutton
2 tbsp mustard oil
2 medium-sized potatoes, peeled and halved
500 gms unripe papaya, peeled and sliced (optional)

Marinade:
2 large onions, chopped
1 tbsp garlic paste
1 tbsp ginger paste
1 tbsp black pepper powder
1 tsp cumin powder
1 tsp coriander powder
¼ tsp turmeric powder
1 tsp salt

Spice paste:
3 black cardamoms
3" stick cinnamon

- Wash mutton, drain thoroughly and cut into 1" pieces.
- Combine ingredients for marinade, rub into mutton and marinate for 30 minutes.
- Soak cardamoms and cinnamon in just enough water to cover, for 30 minutes. Drain and grind to a paste.
- Heat oil in a pressure cooker, add mutton and fry, stirring occasionally till oil separates.
- Mix in spice paste, potatoes, papaya and 2 cups water.
- Close cooker and cook under pressure for 20 minutes.
- Serve hot with steamed rice.

ONLA WANGKHRAI
CHICKEN STEW

Serves: 5

1 kg rice
1 kg chicken
2 drops indigenous soda or ½ tsp sodium bicarbonate
1 tbsp mustard oil
1 tbsp chopped onion
1 tbsp chopped ginger
1 tbsp chopped garlic
2 tsp salt

- Wash rice, soak in water for 10–15 minutes and drain.
- Spread out on a clean cloth to dry completely and grind to a fine powder.
- Cut chicken into 2" pieces, wash and drain thoroughly.
- Place 2½ cups water in a pan and bring to boil. Add rice powder and stir vigorously with a wooden spoon to ensure that it forms a smooth paste without lumps.
- Cook over moderate heat for about 15 minutes, stirring constantly.
- Sprinkle in soda or sodium bicarbonate, mix well and set aside.
- Heat oil in a pan, add onion, ginger and garlic, and fry till golden brown.
- Add chicken and fry for a few minutes.
- Sprinkle in salt and ½ cup water, mix well and cook for about 20 minutes till chicken is tender.
- Stir in rice paste and simmer for 5 minutes, stirring constantly.

KUKURA ARU GAJ

CHICKEN AND BAMBOO SHOOT CURRY

Serves: 5

250 gms fresh or canned bamboo shoot (baans ki kalli)
1 kg chicken
¾ cup oil
2 medium-sized onions, chopped
4 green chillies, slit
2 tbsp Thai red curry paste
1 cup thin coconut milk
1 cup thick coconut milk
2 tsp salt

Garnish:
2 tbsp chopped fresh coriander leaves

- Wash fresh bamboo shoot and soak in water for 30 minutes. Drain, rinse and cut into quarters.
- Joint chicken, wash and drain thoroughly.
- Heat oil in a heavy-based pan, add onions and green chillies, and fry till onions turn golden brown.
- Add chicken and curry paste, and fry for 15 minutes.
- Mix in bamboo shoot and fry for a few minutes more.
- Stir in thin coconut milk, lower heat, cover pan and simmer for 40 minutes, till chicken is tender and dry.
- Stir in thick coconut milk and salt, and simmer uncovered, stirring continuously till oil separates.
- Garnish with coriander leaves and serve.

> **VARIATIONS:**
> Thai red curry paste is available in stores that stock oritental foodstuff.

SOBAI WANGKHRAI
CHICKEN WITH BLACK BEANS

Serves: 5

This is a Bodo dish and is served during special occasions like weddings or when they invite special guests to their homes.

1 kg chicken
1 kg whole black beans (sabut urad)
1 tsp + 1 tbsp oil
1 tsp turmeric powder
1 tsp salt
2 tsp ginger paste
2 tsp garlic paste
3 tsp onion paste

- Cut chicken into bite-sized pieces, wash and drain.
- Clean dal by rubbing with a cloth but do not wash.
- Heat 1 tsp oil in a kadhai or wok, add dal and fry for a few minutes, stirring constantly.
- Pour in 2½ cups water and bring to boil. Cover pan and cook till water has evaporated and dal is tender.
- Sprinkle in turmeric and salt, and remove from heat.
- Cool and grind to a paste.
- Heat 1 tbsp oil in another kadhai or wok till smoking.
- Add chicken and stir-fry for a few minutes.
- Mix in ginger, garlic and onion, and continue stir-frying for 15 minutes.
- Add ground dal, cook for 5 minutes longer and serve.

> **VARIATIONS:**
> **Sobai Jwng Oma Vedor (Pork with Black Beans):** Use pork instead of chicken.

ASSAM

BHOJA HAAH

STIR-FRIED DUCK

Serves: 6

This dish is cooked with fermented black bean paste known as chiakng-pao-ya-ssu, and is available in the markets of Meghalaya and Arunchal Pradesh.

In the plains of lower Assam it is cooked with whole black beans (sabut urad) and the duck is not roasted or smoked.

The dish is also popular in the Lakhimpur area.

1 duck, about 1 kg, pot roasted or smoked
1 tbsp mustard oil
8 dry red chillies, seeded and broken into small pieces
1 medium-sized onion, sliced
1 green capsicum, seeded and shredded
1 small head celery, shredded
2 cloves garlic, crushed
2 tbsp whole black beans (sabut urad) soaked for 30 minutes and ground to a paste
2 tsp sugar
1 tbsp soya sauce
1 tbsp vinegar

- Debone duck and slice into matchstick-sized strips.
- Heat oil in a frying pan, add red chillies and fry for a minute. Drain chillies and discard.
- Add onion, capsicum, celery, garlic and bean paste to pan, and stir-fry for 5 minutes.
- Mix in sugar, soya sauce and duck, and continue stir-frying for 2–3 minutes longer.
- Blend in vinegar, fry for 10 seconds and serve.

KOMAL SAUL
SOFT RICE

Serves: 5

Traditionally paddy is washed and boiled in plenty of water till cooked. It is then drained and pounded lightly to separate the husk. (This can be done in an electric grinder for about 5 seconds.) It is then dried in the sun and winnowed in a large bamboo tray to separate the chaff from the grain. If you use regular rice, this procedure is not required.

1 kg rice with husk (paddy)
200 gms jaggery, grated

- Wash rice and boil in plenty of water till cooked.
- Spread out in the sun to dry.
- Give it a whirl in the grinder for about 5 seconds and separate the husk from the grain to get komal saul.
- Soak rice grains in water for about 20 minutes till tender.
- Drain rice, mix gently with jaggery and serve as a dessert.

TIL PITHA
SWEET RICE PANCAKES

Makes: 30–40 pancakes

This dish is usually served at lunch during the Bihu festival.

1 kg sticky rice
500 gms sesame seeds (til)
250 gms jaggery
Oil for greasing

- Wash rice, soak in water for 1 hour and drain. Spread out to dry for about 20 minutes and grind to a fine powder.
- Combine rice powder with 2 cups water to make a thin batter.
- Heat a tawa or griddle and dry roast sesame seeds till golden.
- Pound coarsely and mix in jaggery.
- Place a kadhai or wok over low heat and grease lightly.
- Spread a thin layer of batter along base of kadhai and cook till base is crisp and upper part cooked through.
- Sprinkle sesame and jaggery mixture along one half, fold and remove from kadhai.
- Serve hot.

NARIYAL KA LADOO
COCONUT SWEET

500 gms freshly grated coconut
1 cup ghee
¾ cup sugar

- Heat a heavy-based frying pan over medium heat and add coconut and sugar. Cook, stirring constantly till sugar melts.
- Remove from heat and place in a bowl.
- Add ghee and mix well.
- Allow to cool and pinch off lime-sized portions of mixture. Shape into rounds and store in an air-tight container.

MANIPUR

Titbits from Loktak Valley

The British were the first outsiders to acknowledge the culinary skills of the Manipuris. In the late 1930s when Surchand Maharaj, the king of Manipur, invited the British to a banquet at his palace, they were treated to a lavish meal consisting of over a hundred and fifty dishes. The vegetarian dishes, prepared by the palace cooks (Brahmins, known for their mastery in cooking), were served on banana leaves in a sumang (a spacious veranda reserved especially for feasts). As the British helped themselves to the sumptuous pakoda thongba (a light curry with gram flour dumplings), they were so impressed that one of the guests wanted to know which tree the pakodé grew on.

Manipuri dishes have not only retained their original flavour but have continued to evolve with time. The people pride themselves on having the largest variety of dishes in their repertoire as compared to the neighbouring states. Known for their love of good food, the Manipuris do not make any compromise with flavour. Even a humble man who can ill afford other material comforts makes sure he gets a good meal. In fact, the Manipuris are the only people of the North-East who have a particular sect of people, the Brahmins, who are hired specifically for cooking at feasts.

Fish is the most popular food here, sixty per cent of which is got from the Loktak Lake. The rest comes from the individual man-made, captive fish ponds (called pukhri in Meitei) owned by almost every household in the state, fish farms and cooperatives. A part of the fish is sent to neighbouring Nagaland, and so during state functions and feasts, they have to get the additional fish from Assam. No feast is complete without fish—dried, smoked or fresh.

Cultural and religious factors are reflected in the gastronomic fare of the people. The Meiteis are devotees of Vaishnodevi and red meat is shunned in their religious festivals and feasts, while for the hill tribes—who constitute nearly forty per cent of the population—red meat is essential for a meal to be complete. So much so, that even an old man will brave the cold to trap a small animal or a bird so that he can at least make a non-vegetarian chutney.

A Meitei woman rises before sunrise, has a bath, and dressed in clean, starched clothes, she applies a chandon tikka (sandalwood mark) on her forehead and enters the kitchen. The day begins with tea without milk and tan (poori) followed by an early meal of steamed rice with kangsoi (a simple vegetable stew) and ironba (a chutney), complimented with fried fish.

Meiteis do not serve non-vegetarian food on all occasions. Fish, for instance, is not served during utsavs (religious feasts) like Mera Mess, etc. During festive occasions like wedding ceremonies, the number of dishes depends on the income and status of the host and could stretch from a hundred and fifty dishes to five.

The Manipuris have evolved their own distinctive cuisine, with kangsoi, ooti, ironba, voksa pok and more. Many of their dishes are flavoured with ngari (fermented fish) and sun-dried fish. Their pickle hawaichar is prepared from fermented soya beans, cooked with sodium bicarbonate. The preparation is drained and wrapped tightly in banana leaves until it matures to a state of pungency.

It is during religious and social functions that the culinary art of the state is showcased. Earlier, Brahmins were engaged exclusively for cooking Meitei feasts. Today they are in demand even with the hill tribes and have to be booked well in advance.

Simple-hearted and hospitable, the people of Manipur consider it impolite if a guest leaves without taking at least a glass of water or a cup of tea. In ancient days, among the Paite tribe, no visitor would leave the home without sipping rice beer. Now tea has replaced the beer and the Paites seldom drink beer. The advent of Christianity has also influenced eating habits. In a dramatic departure from the ancient practice of steaming tanghous (cakes made with powdered sticky rice), today baking cakes is very popular among the Tangkhul Nagas of Manipur.

In a Meitei household, guests who come to stay overnight are very rare. The traditional Meitei houses are large hall-like structures without individual rooms. Family members and helpers dined together and helpers were treated like members of the family.

With the spread of Vaishnavism, the Meiteis slowly discarded their traditional faith Sanamahi, and as a new class of Brahmins was born, society became divided between the Sanamahi and Vaishnavites. The Sanamahi have no idols and they believe that Sanamahi, the household god resides in the south-west corner of each home. While they eat everything, the Hindu Meiteis restrict themselves to fish.

Ningol Chakouba (corresponding to Bhayya Dooj of north India, Bhai Bij of western India and Bhratridwitiya of east India) is a popular festival celebrated on the second day of the new moon of Hiyanggei (October/November), when married daughters come visiting their parents. This tradition goes back to the time when one of the Manipuri kings, who had many sisters was invited for a meal by all of them. He could not attend all their invitations and so fixed a date on which he invited all his sisters. In case the parents are dead, the women visit their brothers' homes, and bring along fruits and sweets. A lavish meal comprising of non-vegetarian food, mostly fish, is arranged. The brothers give their sisters gifts who in turn bless them. Today, some people invite their friends and relatives to show their love and affection. Each member gets a present like a phanek (sarong) and phi (a shawl worn over the blouse). The menu too has changed and the modern Meiteis even serve chicken.

The best occasion to sample the vegetarian dishes of the Meiteis is at their religious feasts called utsavs. Only Meitei Brahmins are engaged to cook and they guard their recipes closely. There are strict dress codes for attending the utsav. Men are attired in white kurta and dhoti and women in a white phi and light pink phanek. The food is served on banana leaves and the guests are invited to be seated by an announcement made in Sanskrit by a Brahmin, a spoonful of salt is served at the side of each plate and another announcement is made. The eldest member, seated at the head of the table or floor takes the first bite and then the other guests start. The first course consists of ooti (lentils), ironba (chutney) and singzu (a salad). This is followed by sagolhawai (black beans or urad in a thick gravy) and then soibum (bamboo shoot), pakodé and paneer cooked in milk. The last course of kheer and seasonal fruits cooked in jaggery is followed by salt. Once again, the guests have to wait for the eldest person to rise, before they can leave the feast.

In festival-related feasts like Ningol Chakouba, Mapam Chakouba, Ngatangba, etc., fish forms the main course with rohu and sareng being the favourites. The service is similar to the utsav feast. Other than rohu and sareng, the Meiteis are especially fond of pengba, khaba, ngaton, ngakra, hilsa and prawn. All preparations are served with rice and not roti which means that almost all dishes have gravy.

They love the bitter taste of suktani (leaves of a bush which grows in the jungles of Manipur), which is served with rice as a starter. The hill tribes round off their meals with milky tea prepared without sugar.

CHI AL MEH
VEGETABLE STEW

Serves: 5

**3 medium-sized potatoes, finely sliced
1 cup shelled green peas or trimmed and chopped French beans
1 medium-sized tomato, chopped
2 tbsp ginger paste
1 tsp salt**

Garnish:
1 tbsp chopped fresh coriander leaves

- Place 2½ cups water in a pan and bring to boil over high heat.
- Add vegetables and cook till tender.
- Mash potatoes with a spoon to thicken gravy and stir in ginger and salt.
- Garnish with coriander leaves and serve.

SANA THONGBA
COTTAGE CHEESE COOKED IN MILK

Serves: 4

1 tbsp oil
2 bay leaves (tej patta)
2 medium-sized potatoes, cut into 2" cubes
3 cups shelled green peas
A pinch of turmeric powder
1 litre milk
1 kg cottage cheese (paneer), cut into 1" cubes

- Heat oil in a pan, add bay leaves and fry till golden brown.
- Add potatoes, green peas and turmeric, and stir-fry for 5 minutes.
- Pour in milk and simmer till thick.
- Add paneer, mix well and serve with steamed rice.

PAKODA THONGBA
CURRY WITH GRAM FLOUR DUMPLINGS

Serves: 4

Curry:
2 cups chickpeas (kabuli chana)
2 tsp ginger paste
A pinch of asafoetida powder (hing)
1 tsp salt

Pakodé:
3 cups gram flour (besan)
½ tsp red chilli powder
¼ tsp turmeric powder
¼ tsp coriander powder
½ tsp cumin powder
1 tsp salt
A pinch of sodium bicarbonate or a drop of indigenous soda
5 flat onion leaves or chives, chopped
Oil for deep frying

Garnish:
1 tbsp chopped fresh coriander leaves

Curry:
- Wash chickpeas and soak in water overnight. Drain and rinse well.
- Place chickpeas in a pan with 2½ cups fresh water over high heat.
- Bring to boil and cook for 20 minutes till tender.
- Drain and reserve water. Use chickpeas for any other purpose.

Pakodé:
- Sift gram flour into a bowl and mix in spice powders, salt and sodium bicarbonate (if used).
- Stir in indigenous soda (if used) and ½ cup lukewarm water, and mix to a smooth batter.
- Mix in onion leaves or chives.
- Heat oil in a kadhai or wok, drop in walnut-sized balls of batter and fry over low heat in batches till golden brown and cooked through. Drain and set aside.

To serve:
- Combine chickpea water and remaining ingredients for curry in a pan and bring to boil.
- Add pakodé, bring to boil again and continue boiling for 5 minutes.
- Garnish with coriander leaves and serve with steamed rice.

MANGAL KANGTAK
GREEN PEA CURRY

Serves: 4

3 cups shelled green peas
2 dry red chillies
1 tsp turmeric powder
1 tsp salt
1 tbsp oil
1 tsp chopped ginger
5 flat onion leaves or chives, chopped
2 medium-sized tomatoes, finely chopped
1 tsp coriander powder
½ tsp fenugreek powder (methi)
½ tsp cumin powder

Garnish:
1 tbsp chopped fresh coriander leaves

- Place green peas in a pressure cooker with 2 cups water and cook under pressure for 5 minutes.
- Open cooker and mix in red chillies, turmeric and salt.
- Cover lightly and simmer over low heat for 10–15 minutes.
- Heat oil in a pan, and add ginger, onion leaves or chives, tomatoes and spice powders.
- Cook over moderate heat, stirring constantly till tomatoes have disintegrated.
- Add green peas with any liquid remaining in the cooker and simmer for 2–3 minutes.
- Garnish with coriander leaves and serve.

OOTI

DRIED GREEN PEA CURRY

Serves: 5

500 gms dried green peas
6 drops indigenous soda or ½ tbsp sodium bicarbonate
1 tbsp oil
1 tbsp cumin seeds
2 bay leaves (tej patta)
3 dry red chillies
2 tsp chopped ginger
3 cloves garlic, chopped
1 medium-sized onion, chopped
1 tsp salt

Garnish:
1 tbsp chopped fresh coriander leaves

- Wash green peas and soak in water overnight. Drain and rinse well.
- Place green peas in a pressure cooker with soda or sodium bicarbonate and 2½ cups fresh water, and cook under pressure for 15 minutes.
- Heat oil in a kadhai or wok, add remaining ingredients except green peas, salt and garnish, and fry till onion turns golden brown.
- Add green peas with its liquid and bring to boil.
- Sprinkle in salt and cook for 5 minutes longer.
- Garnish with coriander leaves and serve.

> **VARIATION:**
>
> **Massori Hawai (Husked Egyptian lentils):** Use husked Egyptian lentils (masoor dal) in place of the dried green peas.

IRONBA
VEGETABLE CHUTNEY

Serves: 6

This is one of the most popular chutneys of Manipur, and accompanies almost every meal.

5 small potatoes, unpeeled
10 French beans, trimmed
3 large mustard or cabbage leaves
5 green or red chillies, ground to a paste
1 tsp salt
2 small fermented fish, lightly dry roasted

- Place all ingredients, except fish, in a pressure cooker with water to cover, and cook under pressure for 10 minutes.
- Drain vegetables.
- Peel potatoes, and mash with remaining ingredients including fish and serve.

SINGZU
MANIPURI SALAD

Serves: 5–6

½ kg unripe papaya
2 tbsp gram flour (besan)
3 dry red chillies
2 small fermented fish
1 tsp salt

- Peel papaya and cut into very thin slices.
- Dry roast gram flour on a tawa or griddle till golden brown. Remove from heat and set aside.
- Dry roast red chillies with fish and grind to a paste with 1 tbsp water.
- Combine ground paste with gram flour and salt, and mix well.
- Add papaya slices, mix well and serve.

> **NOTE:**
> This is often eaten as an afternoon snack or served to visitors.

NGA THONGBA
FISH CURRY

Serves: 6

1 kg river fish (hilsa)
½ cup mustard oil
1 tbsp mustard seeds
½ tsp cumin seeds
1 bay leaf (tej patta)
2 medium-sized onions, ground to a paste
2" piece ginger, chopped
10 cloves garlic, chopped
3–4 medium-sized tomatoes, chopped
½ tbsp red chilli powder
5 green chillies, split
1 tsp salt

Marinade:
1 tsp turmeric powder 1 tsp salt

Garnish:
1 tbsp chopped fresh coriander leaves

- Clean fish, cut into medium-sized pieces, wash and drain thoroughly.
- Combine ingredients for marinade, rub into fish and marinate for 10 minutes.
- Heat oil in a heavy-based kadhai or wok, and fry fish in batches, turning occasionally till crisp and light brown. Drain and set aside.
- Add mustard seeds, cumin seeds and bay leaf to kadhai, and fry till mustard seeds start sputtering.
- Stir in onions, ginger and garlic, and fry till onions turn golden brown.

- Blend in tomatoes and chilli powder, and continue frying till oil separates.
- Pour in 3 cups warm water and bring to boil over high heat.
- Mix in green chillies and gently add fish.
- Lower heat and simmer for 5 minutes.
- Garnish with coriander leaves and serve with steamed rice.

VOKSA POK
PORK WITH MUSTARD LEAVES

Serves: 4

1 kg pork with fat
2½ tbsp rice
500 gms fresh mustard leaves
2" piece ginger, chopped
2 drops indigenous soda or ½ tsp sodium bicarbonate
1 tsp salt
1 tsp red chilli powder (optional)

- Wash pork, drain and cut into 1½" pieces.
- Wash rice and drain.
- Place 2½ cups water in a pan and bring to boil over high heat.
- Add rice, bring to boil again and continue boiling till rice is fluffy and tender.
- Add pork, cover pan and bring to boil again.
- Uncover pan and cook, stirring constantly for about 15 minutes, till gravy thickens with the rice.
- Wash mustard leaves, tear into small pieces by hand and add to pan with ginger.
- Continue cooking and stirring for a further 10 minutes.
- Mix in soda or sodium bicarbonate and salt, and simmer for 5 minutes longer.
- Sprinkle in chilli powder (if used) and serve with steamed rice.

AKSA POK

CHICKEN WITH GINGER

Serves: 5

1 kg chicken
2½ tbsp rice
2 tbsp ginger paste
1 tsp salt

- Clean chicken, cut into small pieces, wash and drain thoroughly.
- Heat a heavy-based pan over moderate heat and add chicken without any water or oil. Keep stirring to prevent it from burning, and cook till the moisture dries out.
- Add 2½ cups water and bring to boil over high heat.
- Wash rice, drain and add to pan. Cover pan and simmer till rice is fluffy and soft.
- Uncover pan and keep stirring till gravy thickens with the rice.
- Stir in ginger and salt, and cook till the aroma of ginger is released.
- Serve with steamed rice.

SANGGOM KHER
MILK AND COCONUT DESSERT

Serves: 4

1½ cups rice
2 tbsp ghee
5 litres milk
5 green cardamoms
¼ medium-sized fresh coconut, finely chopped
4 bay leaves (tej patta)
1 tbsp sultanas (kishmish)
1 tbsp cashewnuts
1 cup sugar

- Do not wash rice. Clean it as well as possible with a dry cloth.
- Melt ghee, mix into rice and set aside.
- Place milk in a heavy-based pan with all ingredients except rice and sugar, and bring to boil over high heat.
- Mix in rice and bring to boil again, stirring constantly.
- Lower heat and simmer, stirring frequently till rice is fluffy and milk thickens.
- Add sugar and continue cooking till it reaches the consistency of a medium-thick porridge.
- Remove from heat, cool and chill.

MEGHALAYA

Delectable Treats from the Khasi Hills

Meghalaya was called the 'Scotland of the East' by the first British colonials who entered the state, because of its scenic beauty, but this sobriquet has nothing to do with the food habits of the people. The people of Meghalaya relish pork cooked with fermented soya beans. Their staple food is rice, and a typical meal consists of a well-prepared pork dish with rice.

Besides rice and pork, if there is one thing that they cannot do without, it is kwai, the local betel nut. In Meghalaya, every family whether lazing around or going about their daily work, do so chewing kwai and reddening their gums in the process. They begin and end their day with kwai. It starts early in the morning, when even a toothless octogenarian is busy crushing the hard betel nut into pieces to keep a day's quota ready. The crushed pieces are then mixed with betel leaves (called tympew in Khasi), tobacco and chemical lime, and the day starts with a mouthful.

The life of the people here revolves around kwai. The first thing they offer a visitor is kwai and if you are served tea instead, it could mean that you are not a welcome guest. Kwai is a symbol of friendship, but a guest is not obliged to have it.

This affair between the people of Meghalaya and kwai is an ancient one and no one knows when it began. There is a legend, as old as the rivers and the mountains of the Khasi hills, woven around two friends who remained faithful to each other to the point of dying for each other. A rich man befriended a poor man in a village and with time their friendship grew and transcended all material barriers. The rich man lavished gifts and food on his poor friend whenever the latter visited him. One day the rich man decided to visit his poor friend, who was at first overjoyed to see him, but was soon overcome with grief, as he had nothing to offer. He sent his wife to buy or borrow some rice, but she returned empty-handed. A pot of water was boiling over the fire but there was nothing to put into it. Ashamed to face their friend, the couple committed suicide. The friend entered the kitchen to look for them, and as soon as he saw their dead bodies, he understood what had happened. He then killed himself saying he did not deserve to live when his loyal friend had given his life. All the while, a thief had been witness to this dramatic affair, and afraid that he would be accused of the crimes, he too killed himself.

Since then, a ritual was born wherein kwai, an economical item, is served in all households. The underlying idea being to bridge the gap between the rich and the poor. Symbols are also derived from this story—the hard betel nut represents the rich man while the leaves are the poor man, the lime represents the wife and the tobacco reflects the character of the thief.

Social functions are incomplete without kwai. In a marriage ceremony, the bride and the groom's family exchange kwai, which reflects the acceptance and extension of their hospitality.

Every meal of all three tribes—Garo, Khasi and Jaintia—begins and ends with kwai. When chewed before a meal it acts as an appetizer, and after a meal as a digestive.

They believe that it retards the aging of their skin (the constant movement of muscles prevents wrinkles) and it is supposed to be the secret of their stamina.

As far as food habits are concerned, the people of Meghalaya are no different from any other North-East tribe, but they have a sweet tooth. They prefer pork to beef or mutton, and there are slight variations in their styles of preparation. Garo cooking is marked by the generous use of indigenous soda in every dish, whether it is the traditional dish, ngakhamkapa (fermented fish) or a pork dish, as it acts as a tenderizer and gives it a unique flavour. The favourite food of the Khasis, is pork prepared with soya beans, and most of their cooking is done without oil or spices, while the Jaintias cook pork with black sesame seeds. Every meal has a simple boiled accompaniment.

In the typical Khasi kitchen, there is provision for smoked meat to be kept around the fireplace. They usually preserve meat or fish for a month.

Although this is a matriarchal society, the kitchen is still the domain of women. Descent is traced through the mother and society bestows more authority to women, but traditionally, men do not cook.

Food has a lot of symbolism attached to it in this society. For instance, during a marriage, the groom and his relatives visit the bride's house carrying rice beer, betel nut, betel leaves and new clothes, among many other items which are handed over to the eldest lady of the bride's family. Food is then offered by the groom's party to the bride's party as a pledge that the boy will not desert the girl.

The marriage ceremony is an occasion for a grand feast. A Christian marriage is solemnized in church after which a feast is arranged by the bride's parents and is attended by both the parties. It is comparatively simpler and less expensive than the Hindu one. Pork prepared with bamboo shoot, ginger, garlic, chillies, etc., is served along with chicken, rice, etc.

On reaching the bride's house, the groom's party is served two gourds of rice beer and betel nuts are exchanged. Dishes of well-prepared meat are then brought out. Rice is served in two or three brass bowls. In olden days, rice beer was also served with the meat.

In ancient days, food was arranged for a departed soul in the belief that it would help the soul on the journey to the village of the dead. After a year, a ceremony called Dapsnem was performed where a rich assortment of food including rice beer, betel nut, betel leaves and chemical lime are offered to the ancestors by the family, for their welfare and that of the clan members. After the advent of Christianity, these practises have been discontinued and modern-day Khasis prefer to have a tea party or hold a grand feast after the funeral.

Apart from the traditional dishes, Shillong is home to more than fifty Chinese restaurants which cater mostly to outsiders. Though they have gained popularity with the local people, they still want their jadoh or liver pulao.

NATHOK BRENGA

FISH IN BAMBOO HOLLOW

Serves: 5

1 kg small fish (rohu or hilsa)
1 tbsp chopped onion
2–3 green chillies, finely chopped
1 tsp salt
A drop of indigenous soda or a pinch of sodium bicarbonate
1 bamboo hollow, 3" in diameter and 5" long

- Clean fish, wash and drain thoroughly.
- Combine fish with onion, green chillies, salt and soda or sodium bicarbonate, and fill bamboo hollow with mixture.
- Seal bamboo with a banana leaf or foil.
- Place bamboo over a charcoal fire and cook for about 20 minutes, till bamboo is almost burnt. Rotate bamboo from time to time to cook evenly.
- Remove from fire and allow to cool a bit.
- Open bamboo and empty contents into a bowl.
- Serve with steamed rice and any other dish with a gravy.

VARIATION:
Use chopped chicken, pork, beef or mutton instead of the fish. In this case it is preferable to partially cook the meat with a minimum of water over low heat, before filling it into the bamboo hollow.

WATEPA

FISH BARBECUED IN BANANA LEAVES

Serves: 6

1 kg fish fillet
1 tsp salt
3–4 green chillies, finely chopped
1 medium-sized onion, chopped
A drop of indigenous soda or a pinch of sodium bicarbonate
3 banana leaves

- Wash fish, drain thoroughly and chop fine.
- Combine fish with remaining ingredients except banana leaves.
- Clean banana leaves with a damp cloth on both sides, dry and pass over a live flame to make them pliable, taking care not to burn the leaves. Cut banana leaves into 5" squares.
- Place 2 tbsp of mixture in the centre of each banana leaf square and fold to form parcels. Tie with cotton string to secure parcels.
- Cook fish parcels over a charcoal fire for about 15 minutes, turning them from time to time for even cooking, till leaves turn brown.
- Open parcels, empty contents into a bowl and serve.

NOTE:
You can use foil instead of banana leaves, in which case make the parcels with 3–4 layers of foil.

The parcels, wrapped in banana leaves can also be cooked in an oven preheated to 180ºC/350ºF for 15 minutes.

VARIATIONS:
- Use chopped chicken, mutton or pork instead of fish.
- You can add chopped vegetables like cabbage or tomatoes to the mixture.
- Papaya flowers can also be added. This enhances the flavour and has good medicinal value for diabetic patients.

NA TOK SHOKAPA
FISH HEAD CURRY

Serves: 4

1 kg fish heads
2–3 green chillies, chopped
2 tsp ginger paste
A drop of indigenous soda or a pinch of sodium bicarbonate
1 tsp salt

- Clean fish heads carefully and cut into medium-sized pieces. Wash and drain thoroughly.
- Place fish heads in a pan over low heat without any water or oil. Cook, stirring occasionally till all water from the fish evaporates and the aroma of raw fish disappears.
- Add remaining ingredients and continue cooking and stirring for 5 minutes.
- Pour in 2½ cups water and simmer till gravy thickens.
- Serve with steamed rice.

NGAKHAMKAPA
FERMENTED FISH CHUTNEY

Serves: 4

2 tsp oil
500 gms fermented fish
1 large onion, chopped
2 tsp chopped ginger
1 tsp chopped garlic
3 green chillies, chopped
2 spring onions, chopped
½ tsp salt
A drop of indigenous soda or a pinch of sodium bicarbonate

- Heat oil in a heavy-based pan over low heat and add fish. Cook, stirring constantly till fish turns soft and becomes a paste.
- Continue cooking and stirring for 5 minutes longer.
- Add onion, ginger and garlic, and continue stirring till golden brown.
- Stir in remaining ingredients and ½ cup water, cover pan and cook for 5 minutes longer.
- This goes well with steamed rice.

VARIATIONS:
You can use ordinary sun-dried fish, but the flavour will not be the same.

WAK PURA
PORK WITH MUSTARD LEAVES

Serves: 4

1 cup rice
1 kg pork
500 gms mustard leaves
2–3 green chillies, broken in half
1 tsp salt
A drop of indigenous soda or a pinch of sodium bicarbonate

- Wash rice, soak in water for 15 minutes and drain.
- Spread to dry till crisp again and grind to a powder.
- Wash pork, drain thoroughly and cut into 2" pieces.
- Wash mustard leaves and shred by hand.
- Place pork in a pan over low heat without any oil or water, and let it cook till water from the pork evaporates and a reddish sediment starts appearing. Stir occasionally to prevent burning.
- As the fat starts melting, mix in mustard leaves, green chillies and salt, and continue cooking and stirring till mustard leaves disintegrate and are well mixed.
- Cover pan and cook over low heat for 5–10 minutes.
- Stir in 2 cups water, cover pan again and cook for 10 minutes longer.
- Blend in rice powder and soda or sodium bicarbonate, and simmer for another 15 minutes till pork is tender and gravy thickens.
- Serve with steamed rice.

WAK AL GALDA
PORK WITH SORREL LEAVES

Serves: 6

1 kg pork
5 sorrel leaves (amrul), washed and roughly torn by hand
2 tsp onion paste
2 tsp chopped ginger
2 tsp chopped garlic
2 tsp green chilli paste
1 tsp salt

- Wash pork, drain thoroughly and cut into 2" pieces.
- Place pork in a pan over low heat without any oil or water, and cook for 20–35 minutes, stirring occasionally till water from pork evaporates.
- Add remaining ingredients and keep stirring and cooking till sorrel leaves disintegrate and are well mixed.
- Stir in ½ cup water, raise heat, bring to boil, and boil for about 15 minutes, till gravy thickens and pork is tender.
- Serve with steamed rice.

WAK ME-A-MESANG PURA

PORK WITH FERMENTED BAMBOO SHOOT

Serves: 6

500 gms fermented bamboo shoot (baans ki kalli)
1 kg pork with fat and bones
2 tsp finely chopped green chillies
2 tsp finely chopped ginger
1½ tsp salt
A pinch of turmeric powder (optional)
½ cup rice powder

- Wash bamboo shoot in lukewarm water and drain.
- Wash pork, drain thoroughly and cut into medium-sized pieces.
- Place pork in a heavy-based pan over low heat without any oil or water.
- Cook for 20–35 minutes, stirring occasionally, till water from pork evaporates and it turns light brown.
- Add bamboo shoot and 1 cup water, and cook for a few minutes, stirring occasionally.
- Mix in green chillies, ginger, salt and turmeric (if used), and simmer till dry.
- Stir in 2 cups water and cook for about 15 minutes till pork is tender.
- Blend in rice powder to thicken gravy and cook for 15 minutes longer.

TUNGRUMBAI

PORK WITH FERMENTED SOYA BEANS

Serves: 6

1 kg pork
2 tsp oil
2 tbsp chopped onion
2 tbsp garlic paste
1 cup fermented soya beans
1 tsp black sesame seeds (til), powdered
1 tsp salt

- Wash pork, drain thoroughly and cut into 2" pieces.
- Heat oil in a frying pan, add onion and garlic, and fry till golden brown.
- Stir in soya beans and pork, and fry till pork is golden brown.
- Add 1 cup water and cook for 30 minutes till pork is tender, adding more water if required.
- Stir in sesame seed powder and salt, and cook for 15 minutes longer.
- Remove from heat and serve.

DOHNEIIONG
PORK WITH BLACK SESAME SEEDS

Serves: 4

1 kg pork
4 medium-sized onions, sliced
2 tbsp garlic paste
2 tsp black sesame seeds (til) A pinch of turmeric powder
1 tsp salt

- Wash pork, drain thoroughly and cut into 3" pieces.
- Place pork in a cooker over low heat and cook for about 15 minutes, stirring constantly, till the fat oozes out.
- Remove meat from cooker and set aside.
- Add remaining ingredients to cooker and cook, stirring frequently till the fat separates.
- Add reserved pork and cook for about 5 minutes, stirring constantly.
- Stir in 2 cups water, close cooker and cook under pressure for 15 minutes.

JADOH
LIVER PULAO

Serves: 7

500 gms pig's liver
3 cups rice
2 medium-sized onions, chopped
2 tsp chopped garlic
1 tsp black pepper powder
1 tsp salt

- Wash liver, drain and cut into 2" pieces.
- Place liver in a pan with 2½ cups water and bring to boil over high heat.
- Wash rice, drain and add to pan with remaining ingredients.
- Bring to boil again, lower heat and simmer till rice is done.

> **VARIATION:**
> This dish is also prepared with chicken liver.

MACHU RASIN CHISIK
BEEF WITH SORREL LEAVES

Serves: 5

1 kg beef
3 spring onions, finely chopped
3 green chillies, finely chopped
5 sorrel leaves (amrul), washed and torn by hand
1 tsp alkaline water (kalchi)—optional
1 tsp salt
A drop of indigenous soda or a pinch of sodium bicarbonate

- Wash beef, drain thoroughly and cut into 1" pieces.
- Place beef in a pan over low heat without any water or oil, and cook, stirring constantly, till water from beef has evaporated.
- Stir in 1 cup water and continue cooking and stirring till dry. Repeat till beef is tender. It should take about 40 minutes.
- Add spring onions, green chillies and sorrel leaves, and fry for a few minutes.
- Stir in 2 cups water, bring to boil and add alkaline water (if used). Lower heat and simmer for about 15 minutes.
- Sprinkle in salt and soda or sodium bicarbonate, mix well and cook till gravy thickens.

MENTIL RITA

RICE CAKE STEAMED IN AN EARTHEN POT

Serves: 6

1 kg sticky rice
1 tbsp powdered black sesame seeds (til)—optional
An earthen pot

- Wash rice and soak in water for 8 hours. Drain and grind to a paste.
- Stir in sesame seed powder (if used).
- Place mixture in an earthen pot and steam for 15 minutes.
- Allow to cool, unmould, slice and serve.

SAKIN GATA
RICE CAKES STEAMED IN BANANA LEAVES

Serves: 5–6

This is usually served as an afternoon snack. It is sometimes taken for lunch while the people work in the fields, as it is very filling.

1 kg sticky rice
A pinch of salt or 5 tsp sugar
3 banana leaves
1 tbsp black sesame seeds (til)

- Wash rice, soak in water for 8 hours and drain. Spread out to dry and grind to a powder.
- Place rice powder and salt or sugar in a bowl and knead to a soft dough with 2–3 cups water.
- Clean banana leaves with a damp cloth on both sides, dry and pass over a live flame to make them pliable, taking care not to burn the leaves. Cut banana leaves into 5" squares.
- Spread about 2 tbsp dough on each banana leaf square and sprinkle over sesame seeds.
- Fold leaves to form parcels, and tie with cotton string to secure.
- Place parcels in an earthen pot and steam for about 20 minutes till cooked.
- Remove parcels from pot, allow to cool, unwrap and cut into slices.

MENTIL PITA
FRIED RICE BALLS

Serves: 7

This dish is served at breakfast or afternoon tea.
1 kg rice
1½ tbsp sugar or grated jaggery oil for deep frying

- Wash rice, soak in water for 8 hours and drain. Spread out to dry and grind to a powder.
- Place rice powder in a bowl, mix in sugar or jaggery and knead with 4–5 cups water to a soft dough.
- Shape dough into egg-sized balls.
- Heat oil in a kadhai or wok and fry rice balls till light brown and soft.
- Serve with tea.

MIZORAM

MIZORAM

Delicacies from the Mizo Hills

Pick any vegetable of your choice and shred it. Heat water in a pan, add the vegetable and salt, and then 'boil top', which means 'just boil it'. What you
    get is bai, a traditional favourite dish of the Mizos. Like bai, the rest of Mizo food is quick and easy to make and they apply their 'boil top' formula to non-vegetarian food as well. A typical special dish for the Mizos is fish or pork cut into large chunks (Mizos love large chunks), boiled in water with salt. This simple form of cooking retains natural flavours in their purest forms. Ingredients are not added to a dish to affect the colour and appearance of the food, and more attention is paid to the nutrient value, natural colour and flavour.

    Earlier, the only known spices were chillies and ginger that grew in almost every kitchen garden. Unlike the other tribes of the North-East, Mizos rarely use ginger for seasoning dishes; fresh ginger sprinkled with salt is served as an accompaniment. It is only recently that it has become a common ingredient in the modern Mizo kitchen. Even today, with easy access to almost all spices, they rarely use them. Spices like turmeric and cloves, and herbs grown in their gardens, are sparingly used. For instance, the Asomiyas prepare alu pitika (mashed potatoes), with pepper, coriander and onions, while the Mizos prepare alu rot, which is just boiled and mashed potatoes with salt. Though the Mizos are non-vegetarians, with pork being the favourite meat, they don't eat a non-vegetarian meal everyday as it is expensive.

Mizos are rice eaters. They begin their day early and the first meal is the tukthuan, or early morning meal at nine o'clock, before they go about their routines. The family gathers around a low-level dining table and seated on moorahs (stools), they say grace. The meal consists of rice, boiled vegetables or fried potatoes and a chutney made of green or red chillies ground with dried shredded meat.

By midday, they gather around the table for chawfak, the midday meal, which often consists of the leftovers from the tukthuan. Sometimes a fresh vegetarian dish may be prepared.

Zanriah or supper is served before sunset, after all the members have returned home. Once again the family gathers around the table, and this gathering together of the family signifies the unity and solidarity that is the bedrock of every Mizo family. In some villages, where the men work in the jhum fields (farms), they return late and the family may have a late supper.

Mizos being Christians, are actively involved in religious activities. Almost every evening they attend church and each day of the week is reserved for a special group, like young men, or married women, etc., to meet.

A typical Mizo kitchen has a huge furnace over which dried meat on skewers and vegetables like beans, mustard and colocasia leaves, neatly wrapped in banana leaves are stocked. A sawm bel (a small container) with fermented meat called Mizo cheese is kept above the fireplace. Paddy is placed in the sun during the day to dry and brought into the kitchen in the evening. The rice is stored in an earthen pot called a fairel bel.

Here too the kitchen was the domain of the woman, and she was rarely assisted by men. Even if the husband happened to be sitting near the fire and the pot was overflowing into the flames, he would merely call his wife and wait for her to stir it. The coming of Christianity has changed their way of life, and the male dominated society is today an egalitarian one where both have more or less equal rights. Still, a woman is expected to exercise her rule in the kitchen.

In the old days, every Mizo family reared animals and poultry for feasts. Even today, pigs and cows are reared in the villages.

Christmas is an important festival. They usually have a ruautheh or community feast to mark the occasion. Like the Nagas, the Mizos contribute generously towards their feasts. Here, men do the real cooking, while the women sit back or help in carrying water or cutting vegetables. Either pork or beef is prepared in a huge pot. For a community meal, banana leaves or well-crafted wooden plates large enough to serve five to ten people are used. The rice is served around the edges and the main dish is placed in the centre.

Mizo society does not discriminate between the haves and have-nots. The rich donate generously for the Christmas feasts, while the poor may or may not contribute anything at all. At funerals, tea is always served without sugar to bridge the gap between the rich and poor. This type of consideration towards the poorer sections of society is typical of Mizo culture. They are a hospitable people and if you enter a Mizo home, you are expected to stay on for a meal or at the very least you will be served tea, which you can't refuse.

MAI AN BAI
VEGETABLE STEW

Serves: 4

20 gms fresh white pumpkin (doodhiya) leaves
15–20 French beans
3 potatoes
5 green chillies
1 tsp salt

- Wash vegetables. Remove veins from pumpkin leaves and shred by hand. Trim beans, peel potatoes and cut into 1" pieces.
- Place all ingredients except salt in a pan with 2½ cups water and bring to boil over high heat.
- Lower heat and simmer for about 15 minutes till vegetables are tender.
- Stir in salt and serve with steamed rice.

MIZO BAI

VEGETABLE STEW WITH MIZO CHEESE

Serves: 5–6

75 gms red pumpkin (kaddu) leaves
12 French bean leaves
2 medium-sized aubergines (baingan) or 1 cup bamboo shoot (baans ki kalli)
2 okra (bhindi)
2 green chillies, chopped
5 gms lengmaser (optional)
½ tbsp rice
1 tsp salt

- A drop of indigenous soda or a pinch of sodium bicarbonate 1 tbsp Mizo cheese (fermented pork) or fermented fish (optional)
- Wash pumpkin and bean leaves thoroughly, remove fibres and tear by hand.
- Cut aubergines (if used) into 2–3 pieces and bamboo shoots (if used) into 2" pieces.
- Trim okra and cut into 2" pieces.
- Place 2½ cups water in a pan over high heat, bring to boil and add all ingredients except soda or sodium bicarbonate, and Mizo cheese or fish.
- Bring to boil again and add soda or sodium bicarbonate and Mizo cheese or fish (if used).
- Lower heat and simmer for 30 minutes till vegetables are cooked.
- Serve hot with steamed rice.

ROTUAI

BAMBOO SHOOT WITH GREEN CHILLIES

Serves: 4

500 gms tender bamboo shoot (baans ki kalli)
50 gms green chillies
1 tsp salt

- Place bamboo shoot and green chillies in a pan with plenty of water and bring to boil over high heat.
- Lower heat and simmer for about 20 minutes till tender.
- Drain and pick out chillies.
- Grind chillies with salt to a smooth paste.
- Cut bamboo shoot into 2" pieces and mix into chilli paste.
- Serve as an accompaniment for lunch or dinner.

ALU KAN
FRIED POTATOES

Serves: 4

1 tbsp oil
1 medium-sized onion, finely sliced
5 medium-sized potatoes, finely sliced
1 tsp salt

- Heat oil in a kadhai or wok, add onion and fry till golden.
- Add potatoes and stir-fry for a few minutes.
- Cover pan and cook for about 10 minutes till potatoes are tender. Sprinkle with water as required to prevent burning.
- Sprinkle in salt and serve with steamed rice and a gravy-based dish.

BAL KAN
FRIED COLOCASIA

Serves: 4

A popular vegetarian dish, served with rice.

500 gms colocasia (arvi)
1 tbsp oil
2 large onions, chopped
1 tsp salt

- Peel colocasia, wash and cut into 1" cubes.
- Heat oil in a kadhai or wok, add onions and fry till golden brown.
- Add colocasia and salt, and fry for a few minutes.
- Sprinkle in a little water at a time to ensure it does not burn and cook till tender and slightly sticky.
- Serve with steamed rice.

MAI KAN
FRIED PUMPKIN

Serves: 4

500 gms white pumpkin (doodhiya)
1 tbsp oil
2 large onions, sliced
1 tsp salt
5 dry red chillies (optional)
1 tsp turmeric powder

- Wash, peel and clean pumpkin, and cut into 1" cubes.
- Heat oil in a kadhai or wok, add onions and fry till golden brown.
- Add remaining ingredients and fry, stirring gently till pumpkin is tender.
- Serve as a side dish.

HMARCHA RAWT
CHILLI CHUTNEY

Makes: 550 gms

500 gms green chillies
2 medium-sized onions, chopped
2" piece ginger, chopped
1 tsp salt

- Place a tawa or griddle over moderate heat and dry roast green chillies till slightly burnt and blackish.
- Grind to a coarse paste.
- Mix in remaining ingredients.

> **VARIATION:**
> This chutney can also be made with dry red chillies. Dry roast chillies, soak in water for 10 minutes, drain and grind.

SA NGA
BOILED FISH

Serves: 4

1 kg river fish (rohu)
1 tsp salt

- Clean fish, cut into pieces and wash.
- Place 2½ cups water in a pan and bring to boil over high heat.
- Add fish and continue boiling till tender.
- Sprinkle in salt and strain.
- Serve fish with rice.
- The stock is relished with rice or served in cups as a soup.

> **VARIATION:**
> Crabs or colocasia (arvi) are prepared in the same way.

NGA KAN
DEEP FRIED FISH

Serves: 7

1 kg river fish (rohu or hilsa)
1 tsp salt
Oil for deep frying

- Clean fish, cut into 2" pieces, wash and drain thoroughly.
- Heat oil in a kadhai or wok, sprinkle salt over fish and fry in batches till golden brown and cooked through.
- Serve with steamed rice and a gravy-based dish.

VOKSA REP
BARBECUED PORK

Serves: 6

**kg pork
1 tsp salt
Bamboo or metal skewers or a flat grill**

- Wash pork, pat dry and cut into 5" pieces.
- Rub salt into pork and thread onto skewers, or place on grill.
- Roast pork over a charcoal fire for 1 hour, turning frequently to ensure even cooking.
- Shred pork, sprinkle in salt and serve with steamed rice.

> **VARIATION:**
> Traditionally the pork was placed over the kitchen fireplace for about a week.

VOKSA CHHUM
PORK RIBS

Serves: 2

1 kg pork ribs
300 gms fresh mustard leaves, washed and torn by hand
1 tsp salt
1 tsp black pepper powder

- Clean ribs, wash and drain thoroughly.
- Place ribs over a smoking fire and smoke for about 1 hour. Cool and cut into 2" pieces.
- Place ribs with 2½ cups water in a pan and boil for 20 minutes till half cooked.
- Add mustard leaves and continue boiling till ribs and leaves are cooked.
- Sprinkle in salt and pepper, and serve hot with steamed rice.

PORK RK-FRY

Serves: 6

This dish has been created by Chef Roukunga, who is currently the only Mizo chef working with Hotel Ashoka in New Delhi. It is a fusion of Mizo and Continental cuisine.

200 gms boneless pork
2 tbsp sticky rice powder
2 tsp cornflour
2 eggs, lightly beaten
1 cup oil

Marinade:
4 tsp oil
½ tbsp vinegar
Juice of ½ lime
4–5 fresh lengmaser leaves (optional), chopped
1 tbsp powdered mustard seeds
1 tsp salt
1 tsp black pepper powder

- Wash pork, pat dry and cut into 4 large pieces.
- Combine ingredients for marinade, mix in pork and marinate for 1 hour.
- Mix rice powder, cornflour and eggs, into pork.
- Heat oil in a kadhai or wok, add pork one piece at a time and fry over low heat for about 20 minutes till crisp, golden brown and cooked through.
- Serve with French fries and boiled vegetables.

> **VARIATION:**
> The dish can also be prepared with boneless fish or chicken.

BONGSA KAN
FRIED BEEF

Serves: 4

1 kg beef
1 tsp salt
1 tbsp oil
1 tbsp ginger paste
2 tbsp garlic paste

- Wash beef, pat dry and cut into strips.
- Rub in salt and set aside for 2 days in the refrigerator to tenderize.
- Rinse beef in water and drain thoroughly.
- Heat oil in a kadhai or wok till smoking. Lower heat, add ginger and garlic, and fry till golden brown, stirring constantly.
- Add beef and stir-fry till brown.
- Stir in 1 cup water and simmer for 30–40 minutes till tender, stirring frequently to prevent it from burning.

VARIATION:
Peel and cut 3 medium-sized potatoes in half and add about 15 minutes after adding beef. Stir in 2 cups water and simmer till beef and potatoes are tender. Serve with steamed rice.

ARSA POK

CHICKEN STEW

Serves: 4

1 kg chicken
1 cup rice
2 tsp chopped ginger
2 green chillies, chopped
1 tsp salt

- Clean chicken, cut into 1" pieces and wash.
- Wash rice and drain.
- Place 2½ cups water in a pan, and bring to boil over high heat.
- Add rice and cook for 10 minutes, stirring constantly.
- Mix in ginger and green chillies, and simmer for about 10 minutes over moderate heat.
- Add chicken and salt, and continue simmering for about 20 minutes longer till rice and chicken are cooked and gravy thickens.
- Serve with steamed rice.

AR SAWCHIAR

CHICKEN PULAO WITH MIZO HERBS

Serves: 5

1 chicken (700–800 gms), kept whole with skin
1 cup basmati rice
1 green cardamom
1 black cardamom 2 bay leaves (tej patta)
2 fresh raja chillies (use any fiery red chillies)
3 stalks celery leaves, chopped
5 leeks, chopped
2 Mizo anthur leaves (use mustard leaves), washed and shredded by hand
1 tsp salt
½ tsp black pepper powder
2 tbsp rice beer (use any white wine)

Garnish:
1 branch parkia, chopped (optional)

- Clean chicken, wash and pat dry.
- Wash rice and soak in water for 30 minutes.
- Roast chicken over a charcoal fire for about 20 minutes, turning frequently till the skin turns brown. (You can roast the chicken in an oven preheated to 120ºC/250ºF for 20 minutes.)
- Cut chicken into 8 pieces.
- Place 2½ cups water in a pan and bring to boil over high heat.
- Add cardamoms, bay leaves, raja or red chillies, celery, leeks and anthur or mustard leaves, and simmer for 15 minutes.
- Drain rice and add.
- Raise heat, bring to boil, lower heat and simmer for 15 minutes till rice is half done.
- Add chicken and simmer for 20 minutes longer till tender.

- Stir in rice beer or wine.
- Garnish with chopped parkia (if used) and serve hot.

> **VARIATION:**
> While you can use any white wine in place of rice beer, the taste will not be the same.

ARSA LLODS
STIR-FRIED CHICKEN

Serves: 4

200 gms boneless chicken
3½ tbsp oil
2 medium-sized onions, chopped
2 tsp chopped ginger
1 tsp chopped garlic
2 green capsicums, chopped
1 cup chopped bamboo mushrooms (use black mushrooms)
1 medium-sized tomato, chopped
3 parkia seeds (optional)
1 tsp salt
1 tsp black pepper powder
¾ cup chicken stock
2 tsp cornflour

Marinade:
1 tsp soya sauce
1 tsp thick red chilli sauce
2 tbsp oil

- Wash chicken, pat dry and cut into 2" strips.
- Combine ingredients for marinade, mix into chicken and marinate for 30 minutes.
- Heat oil in a kadhai or wok, add onions, ginger and garlic, and fry till onions turn golden brown.
- Add remaining ingredients except cornflour, and cook over high heat for 3 minutes.
- Combine cornflour with 1 cup water and add to pan.
- Cook, stirring constantly, till chicken is tender and sauce thickens, and serve.

BUH BAN
STICKY RICE CAKES

Serves: 6

1 kg sticky rice
2 tbsp sugar or 2 tsp salt
Oil for deep frying

- Grind rice to a smooth powder.
- Mix in sugar or salt.
- Add 3 cups water and knead to a soft dough.
- Shape dough into 8" round discs.
- Heat oil in a kadhai or wok and fry rice cakes in batches over low heat for about 10 minutes, turning frequently, till golden brown.
- Serve with tea.

NAGALAND

Recipes from Jhapfu Mountain

The saying goes that the Nagas eat everything that has legs, except tables and chairs. But it isn't really a joke, for the Nagas do relish all kinds of meat with a few exceptions. A typical Naga meal is made up of meat and rice, washed down with zu, the local rice beer. Without zu their food is incomplete. 'What wine is to the Italian, and whisky to the Scotsman, rice beer is to the Nagas. It refreshes him on hot days, encourages him to carry the heavy baskets many hundreds of feet up the steep mountains to the village, loosens his tongue, and makes him merry when on feast days he sits with friends around the fire,' says Christoph Von Furer-Haimendorf, professor of Asian Anthropology, University of London, in *The Naked Nagas*. That was before the advent of Christianity. Today, zu is consumed for traditional reasons during festivals.

The favourite meat of the Nagas is pork or beef, and Naga students living away in hostels keep a stock of smoked meat sent from home. Almost every Naga home in the villages rears animals to be slaughtered at Christmas. Since they do not rear goats, mutton is not a common delicacy.

The Nagas like their food hot and they make it fiery by adding raja chillies and Naga pyaaz or onion. They are not particular about colouring ingredients or other spices. The food is simple: the meat is cut into large chunks, mixed with ginger, garlic, bamboo shoot, Naga herbs and plenty of chillies, and cooked slowly over a wood fire.

The Nagas are simple-hearted, fun-loving people. They loosen their purse strings when it comes to festivals and making merry. With nearly eighty per cent of the population engaged in agriculture, most festivals are harvest-related, but there are also occasions to remember the departed souls, and Christmas, which is their most important festival.

Villages are spruced up and roads cleaned and repaired. Attired in their colourful ceremonial costumes and headgears, they perform traditional dances and songs. Most festivals symbolize equality, so the rich and poor dine at the same table.

Each of the more-than-sixteen-tribes boasts of traditional dishes that vary in style and preparation. For example, the feast of the Ao tribe, which celebrates Oatsu in May and Tsungrem Mong in August, will include ietcgak (bamboo shoot) and amerso (a chicken dish) served with rice and various other side dishes along with the mandatory boiled vegetable called sungoleo.

For the Angamis, the inhabitants of Kohima, the harvest festival, Sekreyni or Phousanyi, which falls in February, represents the protection of life. During this time, men are isolated from women for almost ten days and they carry out all household chores—cooking, carrying water, washing and cleaning—and they do not even eat food cooked by women, who are not allowed to take part in the activities. This is a rejuvenating process to strengthen the men. They drink mahopiva, a specially brewed country beer for the occasion.

Come December, and it's time to mark a successful harvest in the form of a lively festival called Terhunyi. Apart from eating dishes of beef and pork, unlimited zu is drunk from mugs made of animal horns. During this festival, modi, a special kind of pork or beef, cut in large chunks is prepared and served. They also give each other small portions of modi wrapped in paper to display their affection. During weddings, portions of modi are given as return gifts by the hosts.

Almost every Angami kitchen has rows of dry, salted meat over the fireplace throughout the season, which can be preserved for as long as a year.

The Semas, inhabitants of Zunheboto and Wokha district, celebrate Tuluni, a harvest-related festival, in the second week of July. Here the emphasis is on akhuni (fermented soya beans). The Semas relish dishes like awushi kulho (a chicken preparation) and aoshi (a pork preparation).

The Lothas' answer to the Semas' akhuni is bastenga or bamboo shoot, an important ingredient in almost all Lotha dishes. Inhabitants of Wokha district, the Lothas celebrate Tokhu Emong in the first week of November.

The Rengmas, the smallest tribe, live in Phek, and celebrate Ngada in the last week of November or beginning of December. Termed as the festival of zu, the special zu—prepared for the festival—is kept untouched until the eldest male member first tests the beverage. It is customary for every male including baby boys to taste this nye-zengzu while it is prohibited for women. They sit for long hours in the night holding their rice beer in bamboo mugs, chatting and singing traditional songs.

Hospitality is a societal trait of the Nagas that goes with their moral ethos. They love to pamper their guests. No visitor to a Naga house comes away without sharing a meal with the family. In the interior villages of Nagaland, the warmth and hospitality is often manifested by killing a duck or a four-legged animal in honour of their guests. Even the poorest family will bring forth the best it can to entertain its guests. Refusal to dine with them can be misinterpreted as being rude or impolite.

HINKEJVU
COLOCASIA WITH MIXED VEGETABLES

Serves: 5

500 gms colocasia (arvi)
3 cabbage leaves, washed and torn by hand
2 large mustard leaves, washed and torn by hand
10 French beans, trimmed and broken into pieces by hand
1 tsp salt

- Peel colocasia, wash and cut into small pieces.
- Place 2½ cups water in a pan and bring to boil over high heat.
- Add colocasia, cover pan and cook for about 10 minutes till soft.
- Mix in remaining ingredients and continue cooking, stirring and mashing colocasia till gravy thickens.

AKIBIYE

COLOCASIA AND BAMBOO SHOOT POTAGE

Serves: 5

500 gms colocasia (arvi)
100 gms bamboo shoot (baans ki kalli)
1 tsp salt

- Peel colocasia, wash and cut into ½" cubes.
- Wash bamboo shoot in lukewarm water.
- Place 2½ cups water in a pan and bring to boil over high heat.
- Add colocasia and cook for about 20 minutes, till tender.
- Add bamboo shoot and continue boiling till mixture reduces to a thick paste, stirring constantly.
- Sprinkle in salt and serve with aoshi (p. 138) and steamed rice.

ANISHI
DRIED COLOCASIA LEAVES WITH NAGA HERBS

Serves: 4–5

2 dried colocasia leaves (arvi patta)
2 small fermented fish
4 green chillies, chopped
2 tbsp finely chopped ginger
4–5 long aubergines (baingan), sliced lengthwise
3 cabbage leaves or mustard leaves, washed and torn by hand
1 tsp dried lengmaser (optional)
2 tbsp garlic paste (preferably Naga garlic)
1 tsp tangmo (use 1 tbsp lime juice)
1 tsp salt

- Wash colocasia leaves and shred by hand.
- Place 2½ cups water in a pan and bring to boil over high heat.
- Add colocasia leaves, fish, green chillies and ginger, and boil for 5 minutes.
- Add aubergines and cabbage or mustard leaves, and cook for another 15 minutes.
- Stir in lengmaser (if used), garlic, tangmo or lime juice, and salt, and serve with steamed rice.

ITSUK
BAMBOO SHOOT STEW WITH NAGA HERBS

Serves: 5–6

500 gms fresh bamboo shoot (baans ki kalli)
500 gms small river fish (rohu or hilsa)
4 green chillies, chopped
1 tsp salt
1 tsp dried lengmaser (optional)
1 tbsp chopped Naga onion or spring onion

- Wash bamboo shoot and cut into 2" pieces.
- Wash fish.
- Place 2½ cups water in a pan and bring to boil over high heat.
- Add bamboo shoot and fish, and cook for about 10 minutes.
- Add green chillies and salt, and continue cooking till gravy thickens.
- Add lengmaser (if used) and Naga onion or spring onion, and simmer till bamboo shoot is cooked.
- Serve with steamed rice.

GALHO
VEGETABLE STEW

Serves: 7

This dish is usually served in the afternoon as a snack. In the old days, it was taken to the fields for lunch by the cultivators. Today, galho is served as a delicacy in most restaurants in Nagaland.

2 tbsp rice
1 medium-sized cabbage, leaves washed and torn into 1" pieces by hand
5 French beans, trimmed and broken into small pieces by hand
1 tbsp chopped tomato
5 large mustard leaves, washed and shredded by hand
1 tbsp chopped ginger
1 medium-sized onion, chopped
1 tbsp chopped garlic
3 green chillies, chopped
1 tsp salt

- Wash rice and drain.
- Place 2½ cups water in a pan and bring to boil over high heat.
- Add rice, bring to boil again, lower heat, cover pan and simmer till rice is fluffy and soft.
- Mix in remaining ingredients except salt, and continue simmering over low heat, stirring occasionally, till vegetables are done.
- Stir in salt and serve hot or cold.

AKHUNI
FERMENTED SOYA BEANS

Serves: 5

2 tbsp mustard oil
1 cup fermented soya beans (akhuni)
5–6 dry red or fresh green chillies, chopped
1 medium-sized tomato, chopped
½ tsp salt

- Heat oil in a frying pan and add soya beans.
- Stir well and cook over low heat for about 10 minutes.
- Add chillies and tomato, and continue cooking and stirring.
- Stir in salt and ½ cup water, and cook stirring constantly till it thickens to a paste.
- Serve with steamed rice.

NAGALAND

AKHUNI CHUTNEY
FERMENTED SOYA BEAN CHUTNEY

Makes: 2 cups

10 green chillies
2 tsp oil
2 cups fermented soya beans (akhuni)
2 tbsp ginger, finely chopped
1 tsp salt

- Wash green chillies and dry thoroughly.
- Heat a tawa or griddle over very low heat and place chillies on it. Roast till slightly burnt.
- Cool and grind to a paste.
- Heat oil on tawa and add soya beans. Fry, stirring constantly for 2 minutes, till soft.
- Remove from heat, cool and grind to a paste.
- Combine all ingredients and grind once again.

> **VARIATION:**
> Use red chillies instead of green and 2–3 cloves chopped garlic in place of ginger. This can be preserved for days in a refrigerator.

PONGSEN
RIVER FISH CHUTNEY

Serves: 4

250 gms small river fish (rohu or hilsa)
50 gms fermented bamboo shoot (baans ki kalli)
large spinach leaves, washed and shredded by hand
1 tsp salt
1 bamboo hollow, 3" in diameter and 5" long

Garnish:
1 tbsp very finely chopped garlic

- Clean fish, wash and drain thoroughly.
- Combine all ingredients except garnish, and place in bamboo hollow.
- Carefully seal opening of bamboo with foil.
- Place bamboo over a charcoal fire for 20 minutes till the aroma of roasted fish wafts through the air. Rotate bamboo occasionally to ensure even cooking.
- Cool and pour contents onto a plate.
- Sprinkle over garlic and serve with steamed rice.

> **VARIATION:**
> The chutney can also be made with prawns or crab.

THEVO CHU
PORK WITH BAMBOO SHOOT

Serves: 6

1 kg pork
1 cup washed and chopped bamboo shoot (baans ki kalli)
1 tsp ginger paste
1 tsp garlic paste
2 tsp red chilli powder
1½ tsp salt

- Wash pork, drain thoroughly and cut into 2" pieces.
- Wash bamboo shoot, drain and chop.
- Place pork in a pan over low heat without any water or oil and keep stirring for 5 minutes.
- As the pork starts giving out its water, add bamboo shoot. Cover pan and cook over very low heat for 1 hour. Sprinkle in some water if it gets too dry.
- Open pan, mix in remaining ingredients and cook over high heat, stirring constantly for 5–10 minutes.
- Serve hot with steamed rice.

> **NOTE:**
> This is usually served dry but you can add a cup of water with the remaining ingredients, if you want a gravy.

AKSHI

PORK WITH DRIED BAMBOO SHOOT

Serves: 5

1 kg pork
100 gms dry bamboo shoot (baans ki kalli)
1 tsp ginger paste
5 green chillies, finely chopped
1 tsp salt

- Wash pork and cut into 3" pieces.
- Wash bamboo shoot and drain.
- Place 2½ cups water in a pan and bring to boil over high heat.
- Add bamboo shoot and cook for about 5 minutes.
- Lower heat and add pork. Cover pan and simmer for 30 minutes till tender.
- Add ginger and green chillies, and cook for a few minutes longer.
- Stir in salt and serve with steamed rice.

AOSHI
PORK WITH FERMENTED SOYA BEANS

Serves: 6

1 kg pork
1 cup fermented soya beans (akhuni)
10–15 powdered angoithi seeds (use black pepper)
10 dry red chillies
2 tsp ginger paste
2 tsp garlic paste
2–3 medium-sized tomatoes, chopped (optional)
1 tsp salt

- Wash pork and cut into large pieces.
- Place 2 litres water in a pan with soya beans and bring to boil over high heat.
- Add pork and continue boiling for 30 minutes till tender.
- Mix in remaining ingredients except salt, and continue cooking, stirring occasionally till gravy thickens.
- Stir in salt and serve with steamed rice.

TUKULUK LUN
LIVER CHUTNEY

Serves: 5

250 gms pig's liver
2 tbsp ginger paste
2 fresh raja chillies or any other red chillies
10 dry red chillies, lightly roasted and coarsely ground
½ tsp salt

- Clean liver, cut into 1" pieces and wash.
- Place 2½ cups water in a pan and bring to boil over high heat.
- Add liver, ginger and fresh chillies, and bring to boil again.
- Lower heat, cover pan and simmer for 20–25 minutes till tender.
- Drain and grind to a fine, thin paste.
- Mix in dry red chillies and salt.
- Serve hot with steamed rice.

> **VARIATION:**
> This dish is also made with brain.

NASHISHI
BEEF WITH BAMBOO SHOOT

Serves: 6

1 kg beef
250 gms fermented or fresh bamboo shoot (baans ki kalli)
1 tbsp chopped green chillies
3 fresh raja chillies or any red chillies, finely chopped
1½ tbsp finely chopped ginger
1 tsp salt

- Wash beef and cut into 1" pieces.
- Wash fresh bamboo shoot (if used) and cut into 1" pieces.
- Place 2½ cups water in a pan over high heat and add beef.
- Cover pan, lower heat and cook for about 10 minutes.
- Add remaining ingredients, mix well, lower heat and cook, stirring occasionally, for about 30 minutes till beef is tender.
- Serve hot with steamed rice.

TABATHYU
MEAT STEW

Serves: 5

This dish is usually served during the Ngada festival of the Rengmas in November when they are adorned in their colourful traditional costumes, and zu is drunk from bamboo mugs.

1 kg beef, pork or chicken
5 dry red chillies, broken into small pieces
1 tsp salt
2 tsp ginger paste
2 tsp garlic paste

- Clean, wash and cut meat into desired size.
- Place 2½ cups water in a pan and bring to boil over high heat.
- Add meat and boil till tender (40 minutes for beef, 30 minutes for pork and 20 minutes for chicken).
- Mix in remaining ingredients and cook for 5 minutes longer.

CHU HU TATHU
DRY MEAT CHUTNEY

Serves: 5

200 gms dried meat
3 tbsp chopped Angami onion (use regular onion)
7 green chillies, chopped
2 medium-sized tomatoes, chopped (optional)
Metal skewers

- To soften dry meat, bury it in hot ash till you get a burnt aroma. You can also thread meat onto skewers and cook over a live flame for about 15 minutes. Rotate skewers to ensure even heating.
- Clean meat and beat it with a wooden mallet to soften further. Shred meat.
- Grind together remaining ingredients to a paste and mix with shredded meat.

THEVU
CHICKEN STEW

Serves: 6

1 kg chicken
1 tbsp garlic paste 1 tbsp ginger paste
4 dry red chillies, broken 1 tsp salt

- Cut chicken into small pieces, wash and drain thoroughly.
- Place chicken in a pan over low heat without any water or oil, stirring constantly, till water from the chicken dries out.
- Add 3 cups water and remaining ingredients, cover pan and cook for 20 minutes till chicken is tender and gravy thickens.

AWUSHI KULHO
CHICKEN WITH POTATOES

Serves: 5

1 kg chicken
7 green chillies, sliced lengthwise
1 tbsp ginger paste
4 medium-sized potatoes, sliced
1 tsp salt

- Clean chicken, cut into medium-sized pieces and wash.
- Place 1½ litres water in a pan and bring to boil over high heat.
- Add chicken, cover pan and cook for 10 minutes till chicken is half-done.
- Mix in remaining ingredients, cover pan again and cook for 10 minutes longer, till potatoes and chicken are tender.
- Open pan, lightly crush potatoes with a ladle and continue cooking till gravy thickens.

AMERSO
CHICKEN WITH BAMBOO SHOOT

Serves: 6

1 kg chicken
200 gms bamboo shoot (baans ki kalli)
½ cup rice powder
2 tsp finely chopped green chillies
1½ tbsp chopped ginger
1 tbsp chopped garlic
1 tsp salt

- Clean chicken, cut into 2" pieces and wash.
- Wash bamboo shoot and cut into 1" pieces.
- Place 2 cups water in a pan and bring to boil over high heat.
- Add bamboo shoot, cover pan and cook over moderate heat for about 5 minutes.
- Add chicken and cook for about 5 minutes longer.
- Blend in rice powder and keep stirring.
- Stir in remaining ingredients and continue stirring constantly for about 10 minutes, till chicken is cooked and gravy thickens.

TRIPURA

Dishes from the Tripuri Kitchen

For the people of Tripura, food revolves around a fermented fish preparation called shidal. Fish is cleaned, salted, stuffed into a clay pot with mustard oil and stored for about three to four weeks till it matures to a certain stage of pungency. Every household has a stock of shidal which never runs out. Even in the absence of vegetables and meat, they can turn shidal into a hearty meal. Shidal does need an acquired taste, but for the local people, it is used as a taste-maker for every vegetarian dish.

Tripuri fermented fish dishes are really so easy to prepare. Take berema butui—boil some fermented fish and season it with onion and chillies; or chakhui butwi, which uses soda and ginger instead of onion. Serve them with steamed rice, sit on the floor and help yourself with your hand.

Tripuris are rice eaters. They love simple food, just boiled and seasoned with home-grown ginger or chillies. Bamboo shoot is another essential ingredient that accompanies almost every non-vegetarian dish, whether pork or chicken; it is also just mixed with chillies and fermented fish to prepare a chutney.

For the hill tribes like the Reang, Jamatia and Debbrarma, who were once nature worshippers, and are now Hindus, there are no hard and fast rules as far as their diet is concerned. They relish every kind of non-vegetarian dish and rear pigs and mithun (a type of buffalo) for their feasts.

For years these tribes have coexisted with the Bengali migrants from East Bengal. Today, the Bengalis have outnumbered the tribals, but this has not resulted in an exchange of food habits between the two communities, except that the local people have adopted the use of dals and spices. The tribes continue to live in the interiors while the Bengalis live in towns. Like most tribes of the North-East, the Tripuris do not spice their food with condiments. They use just a bit of oil for frying and a pinch of turmeric for colouring. Those who work in the fields have rice early in the morning and come home by noon for lunch.

GUNTOK
VEGETABLE POTAGE

Serves: 5

500 gms of any vegetable (green peas, French beans, cabbage or potatoes)
2 medium-sized onions, chopped
2 tsp chopped ginger
3 green chillies, chopped
1 tsp salt
25 gms fermented fish (optional)

- Clean and cut vegetable of choice, as desired.
- Place 2½ cups water in a pan and bring to boil over high heat.
- Add all ingredients except fish and cook over high heat till tender. Keep stirring to mash mixture and thicken gravy.
- Add fish (if used) and simmer for 5 minutes more.
- Serve with steamed rice.

> **VARIATION:**
> **Rug (Potage of Okra and Green Leafy Vegetables):** Pronounced ruog, it is prepared in the same way using a combination of okra (bhindi), mustard leaves, cabbage and pumpkin leaves, and omitting the ginger.

WASUNG

VEGETABLES COOKED IN BAMBOO HOLLOW

Serves: 4

500 gms bamboo shoot (baans ki kalli)
1 cup button mushrooms
3 bittergourds (karela)
1 cup shelled green peas
7 French beans
3 green chillies, chopped
1 large onion, chopped
1 tbsp chopped ginger
1 tbsp chopped garlic
1 tsp salt
1 bamboo hollow, 3" in diameter and 5" long

- Wash and chop vegetables.
- Combine all ingredients, mix well and place in bamboo hollow. Seal opening with 2 layers of foil.
- Place bamboo over a charcoal fire and cook for about 30 minutes. Rotate bamboo from time to time to cook evenly.
- Open bamboo, drain out liquid that has formed into a bowl and reserve.
- Mash vegetables in bamboo to a paste with a wooden spoon. Pour reserved liquid into bamboo, mix well and empty contents into a serving dish.
- Serve with steamed rice.

MOSODEN
ROASTED VEGETABLES

Serves: 2

**5 small round aubergines (baingan) or medium-sized potatoes
5–6 green chillies, chopped
2 medium-sized onions, chopped
1 tsp salt**

- Roast aubergines or potatoes over a direct flame till skin is charred. You can also place vegetables on a tawa over low heat with a large pan inverted over the tawa.
- Cool, peel and mash to a fine paste.
- Combine with remaining ingredients and mix well.

CHAKHUI
BAMBOO SHOOT POTAGE

Serves: 6

This is a popular dish amongst the local people and is served with rice for lunch and dinner.

1 kg bamboo shoot (baans ki kalli)
2–3 green chillies, chopped
2–3 fermented fish (optional)
2 drops of indigenous soda or ½ tsp sodium bicarbonate
200 gms pork, chopped (optional)
1 cup rice powder
1 tsp salt

- Wash bamboo shoot, drain and cut into 1" pieces.
- Place 2½ cups water in a pan and bring to boil over high heat.
- Add all ingredients except rice powder and salt, and cook for about 20 minutes, till bamboo shoot is tender, stirring frequently. Make sure not to overcook it.
- Blend in rice powder and salt, and continue cooking, for about 10 minutes, stirring constantly.
- The consistency should be that of a thick dal.

> **VARIATION:**
> Use 5 okra (bhindi) and 3 small fermented fish in place of the pork.

AA
FISH STEW

Serves: 4

1 kg fish (rohu or hilsa)
3 green chillies, chopped
3 medium-sized onions, chopped
1 tbsp chopped garlic
2 small fermented fish (optional)
1 tsp salt

- Clean fish, cut into 2" pieces and wash.
- Place fish in a pan with 2½ cups water and bring to boil over high heat.
- Add remaining ingredients, lower heat and simmer for about 20 minutes, till fish is tender and gravy thickens.
- Serve with steamed rice.

AA KARAN
DEEP FRIED FISH

Serves: 4

1 kg fish (rohu or hilsa)
1 tsp turmeric powder
1 tsp salt
Oil for deep frying

- Clean fish, cut into 2" pieces, wash and drain thoroughly.
- Combine turmeric and salt, rub into fish and marinate for 30 minutes.
- Heat oil in a kadhai or wok and fry fish in batches over low heat till cooked through and golden brown.
- This is a side dish and served along with any other gravy-based dish.

CHAKHUI BUTWI
FERMENTED FISH WITH GINGER

Serves: 4

A quick dish that is prepared when they run out of vegetables. It is served for lunch or dinner.

3 medium-sized fermented fish
1 tbsp shredded ginger
A drop of indigenous soda or a pinch of sodium bicarbonate
1 tsp salt

Garnish:
2–3 lime leaves, chopped

- Place 2½ cups water in a pan and bring to boil over high heat.
- Add remaining ingredients except garnish, and boil till gravy thickens.
- Garnish with lime leaves and serve with steamed rice.

BEREMA BUTUI
FERMENTED FISH AND CHILLI POTAGE

Serves: 4

This is a popular item in the villages when they do not have vegetables.

3 small fermented fish
2½ cups water
2 medium-sized onions, chopped
5 green chillies, chopped
1 tsp salt

- Place 2½ cups water in a pan and bring to boil over high heat.
- Add fish and cook till it disintegrates.
- Stir in remaining ingredients, lower heat, cover pan and simmer for about 1 hour till gravy thickens.

WOOKHAN
PORK STEW

Serves: 4

1 kg pork (a good mixture of meat and fat)
5 green chillies, chopped
3 large onions, chopped
1 tsp ginger paste
1 tsp salt

- Wash pork, drain and cut into medium-sized pieces.
- Place pork in a pan with 2½ cups water and bring to boil over high heat.
- Lower heat, cover pan and simmer for 30 minutes till tender.
- Add remaining ingredients and cook, stirring frequently, for 15 minutes longer.
- Serve with steamed rice.

WAK SERJAK
PORK CURRY

Serves: 4

1 kg pork
2 tsp oil
2 tbsp ginger paste
3 green chillies, chopped
2 medium-sized onions, chopped
3 medium-sized tomatoes, chopped
1 tsp salt

- Wash pork, drain thoroughly and cut into medium-sized pieces.
- Heat oil in a kadhai or wok, add ginger, green chillies, onions and tomatoes, and fry till golden brown.
- Add pork and stir-fry till water from pork dries out.
- Stir in salt and 2½ cups water, cover pan and simmer for 30 minutes till tender.
- Serve with steamed rice.

TOKHAN
CHICKEN CURRY

Serves: 4

1 kg chicken
1 tbsp mustard oil
3 green chillies, chopped
3 medium-sized onions, chopped
3 medium-sized tomatoes, chopped
1 tbsp chopped garlic
1 tsp cumin powder
1 tsp salt
1 tbsp chopped ginger

- Clean chicken, cut into 2" pieces, wash and drain thoroughly.
- Place chicken in a kadhai or wok over low heat, sprinkle in oil and mix by hand.
- Cook, stirring constantly till water from chicken dries out.
- Add remaining ingredients except ginger and cook, stirring constantly for 5 minutes.
- Pour in 2½ cups water and simmer for about 20 minutes, till chicken is tender and gravy thickens.
- Stir in ginger and serve with steamed rice.

VARIATIONS:

Musuk Maha (Beef Curry): Use beef in place of chicken.
Punghan (Mutton Curry): Use mutton in place of chicken.

SIKKIM

The Secret of the Sikkimese Kitchen

There are three things that bind the people of Sikkim together: steamed or boiled rice, chhurpi (traditional cottage cheese), and hot, steaming momos. No Sikkimese person will ever disagree that they love all three with equal passion. Every home in Sikkim—right from the far-flung villages to the capital town of Gangtok—cooks these, albeit with slight variations depending on individual taste. These three things are an invariable part of the local cuisine.

Rice is what Sikkimese relish with meat curry, or a simple soupy lentil, or stir-fried seasonal vegetables including mushrooms. Momos are what they will indulge in any time, any day, anywhere. This is comfort food that needs no occasion or excuse, while chhurpi is what adds flavour to their daily diet. It's their all-time-favourite accompaniment that every home lovingly stocks. Even those who are too busy to get into the process of making chhurpi make sure they keep reserves tucked away somewhere in the corners of their kitchens. The cubes of dried chhurpi that are strung together on thick threads are what homesick students studying far away or adults working away from home quietly remember to sneak into their belongings and pop into their mouths each time they long for home.

The people rely on fresh produce from their fields. The availability of crops like wheat, maize and buckwheat has led to the people using them widely in their diets. Millet, for instance, is grown in plenty, and is fermented to make into an alcoholic beverage.

The fermentation of food, be it seasonal vegetables or chhurpi, is a common technique followed by all three communities. In earlier times fermenting food was a necessity. Food was preserved to enable it to last through the long and harsh winter. Everything from spinach to bamboo shoots to soya bean and radish, among other vegetables, was fermented. The tradition is followed, unchanged, to date, despite modern amenities and changes in taste.

The Sikkimese love to experiment with flavours when it comes to traditional chhurpi. They prepare this with assorted vegetables and herbs, and enjoy it with rice. For generations, this cheese has been made by accumulating leftover milk. In the interiors of Sikkim, people usually collect leftover milk in a large pot every day. They store this in hollow bamboo or in big pots. It is collected over a period of time and when it is about 15–20 litres, it is churned with the help of a cylindrical wooden or bamboo churner. It is a painstaking process that takes about fifteen to twenty minutes.

Once the curdled milk has been churned optimally, a jug of cold water is also added to the mix. The liquid is then separated from the solid and all of it is then strained through a fine cloth. It is subsequently let to drain the excess water and stored in containers. Fresh chhurpi is a natural source of nutrients; dried chhurpi cubes, strung on strings, are sold in local shops, and enterprising shopkeepers sell them in small packs. Fresh chhurpi is used to flavour vegetables, used with cucumbers for salads. Locals also use it with wild ferns to lend extra flavour to their food.

The different communities take pride in their own distinct tastes, although it is a combination of collective cuisines that gives Sikkimese cuisine its rich range. The Sikkimese of

Nepal origin are today the ethnic majority. They relish food mostly fried in oil and laced with spices. Their food is far fierier than that of the others, but less spicy than North Indian food. Religion also plays an important role in their choice of food. The Nepalis are primarily Hindus and so they avoid beef, while some sections of the Nepalese eat a pork delicacy they can rarely do without.

For farmers and those who engage in hard manual work, this also revs up the appetite for an early lunch, which invariably comprises rice, dal and vegetable dishes. The Pradhan community amongst the Nepalis is known for their pickles and their typical meat dishes. They pickle almost every vegetable and meat, and their homes are always stocked with them, making them the envy of other communities.

The food of the Lepchas is rather simple but flavourful. It is not high on masalas and spices. The food preferences of these indigenous inhabitants of the former mountainous kingdom revolve around rice and meat, with different, seasonal, locally grown vegetables and produce from the wild, all of which lend a subtle flavour to the food. The food of the Lepchas though flavourful is somewhat bland, as is that of the Bhutias.

Bhutia food is not spicy either. The Bhutias are of Buddhist and Bon descent, and arrived from Tibet around the late sixteenth–early seventeenth century. The first consecrated Chogyal or 'ruler who rules with righteousness (the Law of Dharma)' is said to have migrated from Kham in eastern Tibet in the late sixteenth–early seventeenth century.

The Bhutias love rice, pork, beef and seasonal vegetables cooked in their own distinct style. Momos are also very much a part of their diet. Every kitchen must have an aluminium steamer for making momos, which are prepared with different kinds of stuffings.

Like every community in the region, festivals are the best time to sample the different cuisines in Sikkim. That's when the Sikkimese loosen their purse strings and indulge in feasting.

Come November–December and Losoong—also called

'Sonam Loaar' or Farmers New Year (as it culminates post the harvest festival and precedes the Tibetan New Year falling in February-March)— the Sikkimese celebrate with a food and cultural extravaganza. When cries of 'Tashi Delek Phuntsum Tsog' rent the air, these days, the youth take out boisterous processions on the streets, flinging tsampa powder (roasted flour, usually barley or sometimes wheat flour) in the air. The celebrations go on for about a week, with the real highlight being the first three days. Day one is for immediate family. The locals compete to see who brews the best changkol, a kind of rice beer made from chang. Chang is the traditional drink of the Bhutias and Lepchas and now other communities as well. It is made of fermented barley or millet and served in a bamboo container, called *tongba* in the Nepalese language. Some people also serve tea with milk and sugar, or butter tea for religious or social occasions.

The Losoong festival is preceded by the Kagyed rituals singularly marked by the spectacular tantric dances performed by the monks in their ceremonial regalia of brocade and silk and masks, which represent the various manifestations of wrathful and peaceful deities, the ultimate end of evil and the prevailing of good and righteousness. Come August the Lepchas celebrate Tendong Lho Rum Faat, the age-old religious festival of bringing the community together over the prayer and worship of Mount Tendong, the Kanchenjunga mountain range, and the rivers and caves. The Lepchas believe they were saved from destructive floods by the mountain range and revere it even to this day. The festival falls during the third lunar month every year. The womenfolk prepare a lavish spread of traditional food to mark the occasion.

For the Nepalis, there is no better time than Dussehra and Durga Puja to let their hair down, party and make some wonderful delicacies. This is when housewives make heaps of special breads called syal roti and stock up on it so much that nearly every visitor will be fed this speciality with alu dum and much more. The festival usually falls in September or October.

Food is usually exchanged among the communities during festivals and this is what lift spirits and lends harmony, mirth, gaiety and helps transcend the mundane travails of everyday life.

PAHELI DAL WITH PORK
PORK WITH DAL

Serves: 4–5

½ kg pork
1½ cup whole green lentils (moong dal)
2 tbsp ginger
1 tsp garlic
½ tsp turmeric
3 cups water
Salt to taste

- Thoroughly wash the pork, cut into large chunks, 2–3 inches long, and set aside.
- In a heavy-bottomed pan, boil water and lentils for 10 minutes till the lentils are partially cooked.
- Add salt and spices.
- Stir and gradually add chunks of pork into the mixture.
- Cover and cook on a low flame.
- Occasionally stir to prevent the mixture from getting too thick at the bottom and to ensure it is mixed well.
- Once the pork is soft, it is ready to eat.
- Paheli dal is served for both lunch and dinner with steamed or boiled rice.

KHORSANI KA ACHAR
PORK PICKLE

Serves: 2–3

½ kg pork
½ kg green chillies, whole, with the stems removed
1 tsp cumin powder
4–5 cardamom cloves
1–2 whole cardamom
1 tsp citric acid
2 cups water
Salt to taste

- Wash and cut the pork into 2-inch long pieces.
- Boil the pieces in 2 cups of water and cook till it is soft.
- Once cooked, open the lid and separate the meat from the stock.
- Pour the stock into a pan and add chillies.
- Allow the chillies to cook for about 5 minutes and let the mixture thicken.
- Now, add the cooked pork into the mixture. Stir well.
- Let it simmer for half an hour on a slow fire/flame.
- Add citric acid into the mixture to preserve for about 15 days.
- Serve with rice and other accompaniments. If it is deep-frozen, the mixture can last for 15 days to a month.

SUNGUR KA ACHAR
MEAT PICKLE

Serves: 2–3

½ kg pork/mutton/chicken
½ cup red chilli powder
100 gms cumin powder
5 cloves, roasted and powdered
5 cardamom pods, roasted and powdered
1 tsp turmeric
2 lemons
Oil for deep-frying
Salt to taste

- Thoroughly wash and cut the meat into 2–3-inch pieces.
- Heat enough oil in a pan and deep-fry the meat in batches till it is golden-brown. Set aside.
- Remove half the oil from the pan and set aside in a separate bowl.
- Now, with the remaining oil in the pan, add the spices (chillies, cumin, cloves, cardamom and salt) and shallow-fry over a low flame to prevent from burning.
- Add the fried meat to the mixture and pour the rest of the oil into it.
- Cut the lemons into half, deseed and squeeze the juice into the mixture to preserve.

SYAL ROTI
RICE BREAD

Serves: 4–5

1½ kg coarsely powdered rice (roast any average quality rice and then pound)
250 gms sugar
½ kg butter
4–5 cloves, powdered (elaichi)
1 cup water
1 cup milk
Oil for deep-frying
A pinch of salt

- Mix the ingredients together to make a slightly watery batter.
- Heat the oil in a heavy-bottomed pan.
- Scoop the batter in your hand and gently and carefully put it into the hot oil to make a ring-like design. It needs an expert hand to make that design/shape of a ring.
- Fry till light-brown on both sides. This goes best with alu dum.

ALU DUM
POTATO CURRY

Serves: 4–5

1 kg potatoes
5 masalas (Panch Proran) (Cumin, mustard seeds, saunf, fennel, coriander whole, nigella)
½ tsp turmeric
½ tsp red chilli powder
3 cups water
1 tbsp chopped coriander
Oil for frying
Salt to taste

- Boil potato and peel. Dice and keep aside.
- Heat oil in a pan. Fry the masala including the salt until it sputters, and then stir for two minutes.
- Add the diced potatoes and mix properly.
- Pour water in the gravy and allow it to cook over a low flame until the potatoes are tender; keep the lid covered so the gravy thickens a bit. Turn the flame off once the thickness you prefer has been achieved.
- Garnish with chopped coriander leaves and a squeeze of lemon. Serve with syal roti.

PYAAZ KA ACHAR
ONION PICKLE

Serves: 2–3

250 gms onion
½ kg fresh tomatoes
100 gms ginger
100 gms green chillies
½ tbsp turmeric
1 cup oil
Salt to taste

- Heat oil in pan. Add the chopped onion, green chillies and ginger. Stir well.
- When the onion is golden brown, add the chopped tomatoes and salt and cook until it has a thick consistency. Pair with syal roti.

SUKHA MASU
SMOKED PORK IN BRANDY

Serves: 4–5

1 kg pork
1 cup brandy
Salt to taste

- Clean the pork and cut into long strips.
- Salt it gently and soak it in a brandy overnight.
- The next morning, remove the pork from the brandy and grill over a fire for as long as it takes to cook until dry. (Usually village fires are lit through the day and night and the pork smokes in a week's time. The smoked flavour is what makes it tasty.)

SUNGUR KHUTTA KO ACHAR
PORK TROTTERS

Serves: 5–6

2 kg chopped trotters
Scallions 10 stems
1 tomato, sliced
1 onion, sliced
1 tbsp garlic paste
1 tbsp ginger paste
½ tsp turmeric powder
5–6 sprigs coriander leaves
5 green chillies (optional)
2 red chillies, dried (optional)
1 tbsp oil
1 betel nut (supari) (optional, helps to tenderize the meat)
Salt to taste

- Bring the chopped trotters to a boil with turmeric powder and betel nut.
- Cook on a medium flame for about an hour.
- Cook in a pressure cooker for about 15 whistles.
- When the meat is cooked, drain and remove the pieces.
- Heat oil in a pan. Add the sliced onion and sauté till it is light golden-brown and then add the tomato, garlic paste, ginger paste, chillies, scallions, salt and the trotter pieces.
- Cook until the mixture attains a slightly sticky consistency.
- Garnish with chopped coriander and serve.
- A delicious spicy dish, chewy and gelatinous, this is a popular accompaniment to drinks, and can also be served as a separate dish at a meal, with rice or bhalep (flatbread). The pork can be replaced with beef or mutton.

WACHEEPA
CHICKEN CURRY

Serves: 4–5

1 chicken, whole (preferably country chicken)
1 kg rice
4 onions
12 green chillies (optional)
2 cups shredded ginger
250 gms oil
2 glasses water (enough to drown the rice and cook)
Salt to taste

- Dress the chicken clean by plucking the feathers off completely.
- Sear or burn the dressed chicken over an open fire and keep flipping sides in order to prevent it from getting too burnt. Scrape the chicken clean.
- Set aside a small handful of the scraped soft feathers.
- Cut the chicken, with its bones, into fingernail-sized pieces.
- Heat oil. Add sliced onions, ginger, green chillies and chopped chicken.
- Stir-fry the mixture and let it cook for 10 minutes.
- Add the scraped feathers and let it simmer for five minutes.
- Add the washed rice and mix well. Add the water and cook till it becomes like a pulao.

PATSA DOH

BAMBOO SHOOTS WITH COTTAGE CHEESE

Serves: 2–3

300 gms bamboo shoot
1 cup cottage cheese
½ tsp cumin seeds
½ tsp mustard seeds
½ tsp turmeric powder
2 green chillies (optional)
1 tbsp oil
Salt to taste

- Peel and slice the bamboo shoots. Set aside.
- Heat oil in a pan. Add cumin, mustard seeds and turmeric powder. Once it splutters, stir to prevent from burning at the bottom.
- Add the chopped bamboo pieces and fry for a few minutes. (Fresh shoots may take longer than tinned ones.)
- Allow the bamboo shoots to cook on medium fire for about 10 minutes.
- When tender, add cottage cheese and chillies and let it simmer to a semi-dry state. Serve hot with rice or bread.

KHOODI

BUCKWHEAT ROLL WITH SPINACH-AND-CHEESE STUFFING

Serves: 3–4

½ kg buckwheat flour
2 cups water
1 kg spinach or any other green seasonal vegetables, chopped, washed and wiped dry
350 gms cottage cheese
1 onion, thinly sliced
2 tomatoes, chopped
2 tsp oil
A pinch of turmeric

- Make a batter of the buckwheat with water and spread on a non-stick pan over medium flame, as you would a pancake. Make sure there is no oil. Once the pancakes are done, set them aside.
- Heat oil in a pan. Add the onion and tomatoes and stir till the mixture becomes a coarse paste.
- Add the pinch of turmeric. Then add the chopped spinach and let it cook for a while and, when it's almost done, add the cottage cheese.
- Continue to stir and keep frying till it turns light golden-brown.
- Take buckwheat pancake, place a spoonful of the stuffing on it, and roll it up as if making an egg roll.
- To reheat before serving, either steam or microwave.
- *Khoo* in Sikkimese means 'bread' and *di* means 'to roll'. Khoodi is a stuffed bread-roll. This is a popular dish of the Lepcha tribes in Sikkim, usually prepared by housewives and served as a snack at teatime.

MINCHA TSAM-THU
MILLET PORRIDGE

Serves: 2

1 cup millet flour
2 tbsp butter
1 egg, beaten
1 cup water
Salt to taste

- Melt some butter in a small pan and add the beaten egg to it. Let it fry for a minute.
- Add the millet flour to the fried egg and gently stir to mix well as if making scrambled eggs.
- Add boiling hot water to the mix to get a porridge-like consistency.
- The Bhutia tribes of Sikkim specially love this preparation. It can be served for breakfast or in the afternoon to kill mid-evening hunger pangs.

SOCHHA PATSA TSOEM
NETTLE SOUP WITH BAMBOO SHOOT

Serves: 2–3

½ kg beef
1 onion, chopped
1 tomato, chopped
250 gms bamboo shoot
250 gms nettle leaves
5 cups water (approx.)
Oil to fry

- Wash and mince the beef and set aside.
- Heat oil in a pan. Add chopped onion and tomatoes, followed by minced beef. Stir.
- Continue to stir and, when the moisture dries up, add a cup of hot water and let it cook over low flame.
- Cover it with a lid till the water dries up. Stir occasionally to make sure it does not burn.
- When the meat is tender, add the bamboo shoots and continue cooking over low heat.
- Add more water (2–3 cups) and nettle leaves (washed clean).
- Boil for three to four minutes more and serve.
- This is a typical Bhutia specialty, usually eaten as a between-meals afternoon soup. It can also be a good appetizer both for lunch or dinner.

SHYA-PHALEY

BREAD WITH MEAT FILLING

Serves: 3–4

½ kg cornflour
½ kg pork/beef/chicken
250 gms onion, chopped
5 medium-sized tomatoes, chopped
2 tbsp ginger paste
Salt to taste

- Heat oil in a pan and add onions, tomatoes and ginger paste.
- Stir till it becomes a fine paste and add chopped meat of your choice. When it is done, keep aside.
- Now, make a dough out of the cornflour, like the dough for chapattis, and make small puris.
- Fill the puris with a spoonful of the fried beef and seal it with your finger as if making momos (see recipe on p. 20).
- Deep-fry them (shya-phaleys) in batches till light brown. Serve with chutney.
- The Bhutia tribes of Sikkim usually prepare this for guests and visiting relatives. It is sometimes served as an appetizer or an afternoon snack.

SHAMO

SAUTÉED SEASONAL MUSHROOM

Serves: 2–3

250 gms seasonal mushroom (any)
2 tbsp butter
Salt to taste

- Gently wash the mushrooms and keep aside. Make it free from moisture. Slice as desired.
- Meanwhile, heat butter in a frying pan and add the mushrooms. Add salt and it is ready to serve.

PHAKSHA
PORK CURRY

Serves: 2–3

½ kg pork
½ tsp turmeric
50 gms fresh bamboo shoot
50 gms ginger, shredded
Salt to taste

- Wash and cut the pork into 2–3-inch pieces and boil in a pan with shredded ginger.
- When the liquid begins to dry up, add the bamboo shoots, salt and turmeric.
- When the pork is tender, it is ready to serve.

SHACHU
DRIED BEEF

Serves: 4–5

1 kg beef
2 tsp turmeric
Salt to taste

- Wash the beef and cut into long strips.
- Salt and drape strips over a stick, like clothes hung out to dry. Leave the meat by a wood fire indoors, or in the sun to dry, and, in the process, cook. It should take about a month.
- When it is done, cut the dried beef into pieces. It can then be sautéed or added into any soup for flavouring.

DOLUM

CHHURPI OR COTTAGE CHEESE WITH BRINJAL

Serves: 2–3

250 gms cottage cheese
6 long brinjals, cut long
1 tsp turmeric
1 tomato
1 onion
Salt to taste

- Heat oil in a pan and fry onion till golden.
- Add the brinjal, cottage cheese and tomato and stir till the brinjal is cooked.

CHUMTHUK
RICE GRUEL

Serves: 2

250 gms starchy rice
2 tsp ginger, shredded
100 gms beef, finely chopped for flavouring
3–4 cups water for cooking

- Mix the rice into the pot of water and add the rest of the ingredients. Cover for five minutes.
- Open the lid and stir constantly to prevent from getting stuck at the bottom.
- Cook until the meat is tender. Make sure that it has a soupy consistency. This is an ideal afternoon meal.

THAMPA
ROASTED RICE POWER

Serves: 2

250 gms rice (or more as desired)
2 tsp clarified butter (or more)
Salt/sugar/honey to taste

- Roast the rice in a thick-bottomed pan. Let it cool and then pound to make a fine powder.
- Add clarified butter and sugar or salt and mix well.
- This is a popular breakfast or mid-morning snack. The roasted powder can also be stored in an airtight container and preserved for about a month.

PATSO
STEAMED FISH IN A BAMBOO HOLLOW

Serves: 3–4

1 kg small river fish
1 tsp turmeric
1 tomato, chopped
1 onion, finely chopped
1 tbsp mustard oil
Fresh hollow bamboo for steaming
Salt to taste

- Clean the fish thoroughly and apply mustard oil as if marinating.
- Mix the rest of the ingredients together. Put the mixture inside a hollow bamboo.
- Seal the open end with banana leaf.
- Put the bamboo near a fire to roast it. Keep turning it for about 15–20 minutes to ensure it is evenly cooked.

Glossary

English	Hindi
Almond	Badam
Asafoetida	Hing
Aubergine	Baingan
Bamboo shoot	Baans ki kalli
Bay leaf	Tej patta
Beef	Gai ka gosht
Bengal gram flour	Besan
Betel leaf	Paan
Betel nut	Supari
Bittergourd	Karela
Black beans	
– Husked	Urad dal
– Whole	Sabut urad
Black pepper	Kali mirch
Bottlegourd	Ghia/lauki
Brain	Bheja
Cabbage	Band gobhi
Capsicum	Shimla mirch
Cardamom	
– Black	Badi elaichi
– Green	Hari elaichi/chhoti elaichi

English	Hindi
Carp	Rohu
Carrot	Gaajar
Cashewnut	Kaju
Cauliflower	Phool gobhi
Celery	Selery
Chicken	Murgh
Chickpeas	Kabuli channa/safaid channa
Chilli	Mirchi
– Dried, red	Sookhi mirch
– Green	Hari mirch
– Red	Lal mirch
Cinnamon	Dalchini
Coconut	
– Fresh	Nariyal
– Milk	Nariyal ka doodh
Colocasia	Arvi
– Leaves	Arvi patta
Coriander	
– Fresh	Hara dhania
– Seeds	Sabut dhania
Cottage cheese	Paneer
Crab	Kekda
Cumin seeds	Jeera
Curd	Dahi
Duck	Badak
Egg	Anda
Egyptian lentils	
– Husked	Masoor dal
– Whole	Sabut masoor
Fenugreek seeds	Methi dana
Fish	Machchi/Machchli
French beans	Fransbin
Garlic	Lehsun
Ginger	
– Fresh	Adrak

English	Hindi
Gooseberry	Rashbari
Green peas	Mattar
Jaggery	Gurd
Leeks	Vilaiti pyaaz
Lentils	Dal
Lime	Limbu/nimbu
Liver	Kaleji
Milk	Doodh
Mince	Keema
Mushroom	Dhingri/khumi Mustard
– Greens	Sarson ka saag
– Oil	Sarson ka tel
– Seeds	Sarson/rai
Mutton	Gosht
Oil Tel	
Okra	Bhindi
Onion	Pyaaz
Papaya	
– Unripe	Kaccha papeeta
Peppercorn	Kali mirch
Pork	Suvar ka gosht
Potato	Alu
Prawn	Jhinga
Pumpkin	
– White	Doodhiya
– Red/yellow	Seetaphul/kaddu Radish
– White	Safaid mooli
Rice	Chaval
Salt	Namak
Sesame seeds	Til
Shad	Hilsa
Shrimp	Jhinga/kolmi
Sodium bicarbonate	Meetha soda
Sorrel	Amrul
Spinach	Palak

English	Hindi
Spring onions	Hara pyaaz
Sugar	Cheeni/shakkar
Sultana	Kishmish
Tamarind	Imli
Tomato	Tamatar
Turmeric	Haldi
Vinegar	Sirka
Wheat	
– Plain/refined flour	Maida

NOTE:
The following ingredients are found only in the North-East and have been described in the introduction under 'Speciality Ingredients':

Akhuni, Angoithi seeds, Bamboo mushrooms, Indigenous soda, Lengmaser, Mizo anthur, Parkia, Raja chillies, Repchi, Sticky rice, Tangmo.

Index

BEEF
Bongsa kan (Fried beef) 116
Chow-chow (Noodles with meat and vegetables) 16
Chu hu tathu (Dry meat chutney) 142
Goru adin (Stir-fried beef) 14
Machu rasin chisik (Beef with sorrel leaves) 94
Momos 20
Musuk maha (Beef curry) 161
Nashishi (Beef with bamboo shoot) 140
Tabathyu (Meat stew) 141
Shya-phaley (Bread with meat filling) 183
Shachu (Dried beef) 186

CHICKEN
Aksa pok (Chicken with ginger) 74
Amerso (Chicken with bamboo shoot) 145
Amin oying (Chicken stew) 17
Ar sawchiar (Chicken pulao with Mizo herbs) 118
Arsa llods (Stir-fried chicken) 120
Arsa pok (Chicken stew) 117
Awushi kulho (Chicken with potatoes) 144
Chow-chow (Noodles with meat and vegetables) 16
Etoh (Chicken stew with ginger) 18
Kukura aru gaj (Chicken and bamboo shoot curry) 50
Momos 20

Onla wangkhrai (Chicken stew)   49
Shya-phaley (Bread with meat filling)
Sobai wangkhrai (Chicken with black beans)   51
Sungur ka achar (Meat pickle)   172
Tabathyu (Meat stew)   141
Thevu (Chicken stew)   143
Tokhan (Chicken curry)   161
Wacheepa (Chicken curry)   178

CHUTNEYS AND PICKLES
Akhuni chutney (Fermented soya bean chutney)   134
Chu hu tathu (Dry meat chutney)   142
Ironba (Vegetable chutney)   69
Khorsani ka achar (Pork pickle)   171
Luktar (Dried pork and bamboo shoot pickle)   13
Hmarcha rawt (Chilli chutney)   110
Napham bathun (Fermented fish chutney)   35
Ngakhamkapa (Fermented fish chutney)   87
Pongsen (River fish chutney)   135
Pyaaz ka achar (Onion pickle)   175
Rongpu takeng (Egg chutney)   19
Sungur ka achar (Meat pickle)   172
Tukuluk lun (Liver chutney)   139

DESSERTS AND SWEETS
Nariyal ka ladoo (Coconut sweet)   55
Sanggom kher (Milk and coconut dessert)   75
Til pitha (Sweet rice pancakes)   54

DUCK
Bhoja haah (Stir-fried duck)   52

EGGS
Rongpu takeng (Egg chutney)   19

FISH
Aa (Fish stew)   155
Aa karan (Deep fried fish)   156
Asin puinam (Fish in bamboo hollow)   10
Berema butui (Fish and chilli potage)   158
Chakhui butwi (Fish with ginger)   157

Khar—II (Bottlegourd with fish) 33
Maas patotia (Fish roasted in banana leaves) 36
Maas-patot-dia (Fish baked in banana leaves) 37
Masor jhol—I (Fish curry) 39
Masor jhol—II (Fish curry) 41
Masor tenga (Sour fish) 43
Napham (Fish with colocasia leaves) 34
Patso (Steamed fish in a bamboo hollow) 190
Napham bathun (Fermented fish chutney) 35
Na tok shokapa (Fish head curry) 86
Ngakhamkapa (Fermented fish chutney) 87
Nathok brenga (Fish in bamboo hollow) 83
Nga kan (Deep fried fish) 112
Nga thongba (Fish curry) 71
Pongsen (River fish chutney) 135
Sa nga (Boiled fish) 111
Watepa (Fish barbecued in banana leaves) 84

GRAINS

Bread:
– Syal roti (Rice bread) 173
– Khoodi (Buckwheat roll with spinach-and-cheese stuffing) 180
– Shya-phaley (Bread with meat filling) 183

Porridge:
– Mincha tsam-thu (Millet porridge) 181

MUTTON
Aso adin (Mutton stew with ginger) 15
Chow-chow (Noodles with meat and vegetables) 16
Mansha jhol (Mutton curry) 48
Punghan (Mutton curry) 161
Tabathyu (Meat stew) 141
Sungur ka achar (Meat pickle) 172

PORK
Akshi (Pork with dried bamboo shoot) 137
Aoshi (Pork with fermented soya beans) 138
Arek (Pork stew with bamboo shoot) 12
Chow-chow (Noodles with meat and vegetables) 16

Chu hu tathu (Dry meat chutney) 142
Dohneiiong (Pork with black sesame seeds) 92
Ili (Pork stew with ginger) 11
Jadoh (Liver pulao) 93
Khorsani ka achar (Pork pickle) 171
Luktar (Dried pork and bamboo shoot pickle) 13
Momos 20
Oma bedor saonai (Barbecued pork) 45
Oma eonai (Fried pork) 46
Oma vedor gwran (Sun-dried pork) 47
Paheli dal with pork (Pork with dal) 170
Phaksha (Pork curry) 185
Pork RK-fry 115
Shya-phaley (Bread with meat filling) 183
Sobai jwng oma vedor (Pork with black beans) 51
Sukha masu (Smoked pork in brandy) 176
Sungur ka achar (Meat pickle) 172
Sungur khutta ko achar (Pork trotters) 177
Tabathyu (Meat stew) 141
Thevo chu (Pork with bamboo shoot) 136
Tukuluk lun (Liver chutney) 139
Tungrumbai (Pork with fermented soya beans) 91
Voksa chhum (Pork ribs) 114
Voksa pok (Pork with mustard leaves) 73
Voksa rep (Barbecued pork) 113
Wak al galda (Pork with sorrel leaves) 89
Wak me-a-mesang pura (Pork with fermented bamboo shoot) 90
Wak pura (Pork with mustard leaves) 88
Wak serjak (Pork curry) 160
Wookhan (Pork stew) 159

RICE
Ar sawchiar (Chicken pulao with Mizo herbs) 118
Buh ban (Sticky rice cakes) 121
Chumthuk (Rice gruel) 188
Ething (Rice cake steamed in banana leaves) 21
Jadoh (Liver pulao) 93
Komal saul (Soft rice) 53
Mentil pita (Fried rice balls) 97
Mentil rita (Rice cake steamed in an earthen pot) 95

Sakin gata (Rice cakes steamed in banana leaves) 96
Thampa (Roasted rice power) 189
Til pitha (Sweet rice pancakes) 54

TEA
Ts-ja (Tea with yak's milk) 22

VEGETABLES

Bamboo shoot:
- Akibiye (Colocasia and bamboo shoot potage) 129
- Chakhui (Bamboo shoot potage) 154
- Ekung (Tender bamboo shoot with chillies) 9
- Itsuk (Bamboo shoot stew with Naga herbs) 131
- Patsa doh (Bamboo shoots with cottage cheese) 179
- Rotuai (Bamboo shoot with green chillies) 106
- Sochha patsa tsoem (nettle soup with bamboo shoot) 182

Bottlegourd (lauki):
- Khar—II (Bottlegourd with fish) 33

Chillies:
- Hmarcha rawt (Chilli chutney) 110

Colocasia (arvi):
- Akibiye (Colocasia and bamboo shoot potage) 129
- Anishi (Dried colocasia leaves with Naga herbs) 130
- Bal kan (Fried colocasia) 108
- Hinkejvu (Colocasia with mixed vegetables) 128
- Kosu hajor (Sour colocasia leaf curry) 30

Cottage cheese (paneer):
Dolum (Chhurpi or cottage cheese with brinjal) 187
Patsa doh (Bamboo shoots with cottage cheese) 179
- Sana thongba (Cottage cheese cooked in milk) 64

Green peas:
- Mangal kangtak (Green pea curry) 67
- Ooti (Dried green pea curry) 68

Lentils (dal):
- Khar—I (Black beans with unripe papaya) 32

INDEX 199

- Massori hawai (husked Egyptian lentils) 68
- Mati dal (Black beans with pumpkin) 31
- Pakoda thongba (Curry with gram flour dumplings) 65

Mixed Vegetables:
- Chi al meh (Vegetable stew) 63
- Galho (Vegetable Stew) 132
- Guntok (Vegetable potage) 151
- Hinkejvu (Colocasia with mixed vegetables) 128
- Ironba (Vegetable chutney) 69
- Mai an bai (Vegetable stew) 104
- Mizo bai (Vegetable stew with Mizo cheese) 105
- Mosoden (Roasted vegetables) 153
- Oying (Vegetable stew) 7
- Rug (Potage of okra and green leafy vegetables) 151
- Singzu (Manipuri salad) 70
- Thukpa (Vegetable stew with noodles) 8
- Wasung (Vegetables cooked in bamboo hollow) 152

Mushrooms:
- Shamo (Sautéed seasonal mushroom) 184

Onions:
- Pyaaz ka achar (Onion pickle) 175

Potatoes:
- Alu dum (Potato curry) 174
- Alu kan (Fried potatoes) 107
- Alu pitika (Spicy mashed potatoes) 29

Pumpkin (doodhya):
- Mai kan (Fried pumpkin) 109
- Mati dal (Black beans with pumpkin) 31

Soya beans:
- Akhuni (Fermented soya beans) 133
- Akhuni chutney (Fermented soya bean chutney) 134